Ready to Present
A Guide to Better Presentations

Herman Bartelen / Malcolm Kostiuk

Australia · Brazil · Mexico · Singapore · United Kingdom · United States

Ready to Present—A Guide to Better Presentations

Herman Bartelen / Malcolm Kostiuk

© 2019 Cengage Learning K.K.

ALL RIGHTS RESERVED. No part of this work covered by the copyright herein may be reproduced, transmitted, stored, or used in any form or by any means—graphic, electronic, or mechanical, including but not limited to photocopying, recording, scanning, digitizing, taping, Web distribution, information networks, or information storage and retrieval systems—without the prior written permission of the publisher.

"National Geographic", "National Geographic Society" and the Yellow Border Design are registered trademarks of the National Geographic Society ® Marcas Registradas

Photo Credits:
p. 9: © Steve Debenport/iStock.com; p. 10: (t) © stockstudioX/iStock.com, (m) © claudio.arnese/iStock.com, (b) © PeopleImages/iStock.com; p. 17: © LightFieldStudios/iStock.com; p. 18: (t) © scoutgirl/iStock.com, (b) © urbancow/iStock.com; p. 25: (t) © MStudioImages/iStock.com, (t, l to r) © noririn/iStock.com, © RomoloTavani/iStock.com, (m, l to r) © twinsterphoto/iStock.com, © ElenaNichizhenova/iStock.com, (b, l to r) © stock_colors/iStock.com, © VanWyckExpress/iStock.com; p. 26 (t) & p. 30 (b): © ©FabianLeow/iStock.com; p. 26: (b) © Herman Bartelen; p. 33: © ViewApart/iStock.com; p. 34: (t) © Wachiwit/iStock.com, (b) © AlekZotoff/iStock.com; p. 43: (t, l to r) © Dave Benett/Hulton Archive/Getty Images, © The Asahi Shimbun/The Asahi Shimbun/Getty Images, © The Asahi Shimbun/The Asahi Shimbun/Getty Images, (b, l to r) © Bettmann/Bettmann/Getty Images, © Justin Sullivan/Getty Images News/Getty Images, © Archives21 (RM)/Pacific Press Service; p. 44: (t) © Fine Art/Corbis Historical/Getty Images, (b) © Fine Art/Corbis Historical/Getty Images; p. 51: © FatCamera/iStock.com; p. 52: (t) © TAGSTOCK1/iStock.com, (b) © KatarzynaBialasiewicz/iStock.com; p. 59: © DuxX/iStock.com; p. 60: (t) © apomares/iStock.com, (b) ANNECORDON/iStock.com; p. 67: © jeffbergen/iStock.com; p. 68: (t) © guenterguni/iStock.com, (m) © ugurhan/iStock.com, (b) © hadynyah/iStock.com; p. 86: © SolStock/iStock.com, © Dimitris66/iStock.com; p. 90: (t) © Jodi Jacobson/iStock.com; p. 92: (t) © Choreograph/iStock.com, (b) © Hung_Chung_Chih/iStock.com; p. 93: (t) © LUNAMARINA/iStock.com, (b) © erhui1979/iStock.com; p. 94: © MarkPapas/iStock.com; p. 95: (t) © A-Digit/iStock.com, (b) © mediaphotos/iStock.com; p. 96: (t) © scyther5/iStock.com, (b) © Mauricio Graiki/iStock.com; p. 97: (t) © cozyta/iStock.com, (b) © studio023/iStock.com; p. 98: (t) © PeopleImages/iStock.com, (m) © Squaredpixels/iStock.com, (b, l to r) © urbazon/iStock.com, © nd3000/iStock.com, © mediaphotos/iStock.com

Unless noted above, all photos are from the *Ready to Present* Video Program: © Cengage Learning K.K.

For permission to use material from this textbook or product, e-mail to **eltjapan@cengage.com**

ISBN: 978-4-86312-351-9

National Geographic Learning | Cengage Learning K.K.
No. 2 Funato Building 5th Floor
1-11-11 Kudankita, Chiyoda-ku
Tokyo 102-0073
Japan

Tel: 03-3511-4392
Fax: 03-3511-4391

Acknowledgments:
The authors and publisher would like to thank the following for their cooperation in filming for this textbook: (In alphabetical order) Rinka Hayashida; Shohei Otaki; Sina Takada; Masumi Yamaike

Table of Contents

Scope and Sequence — 4
Introduction — 6
How to access the video and audio online — 8

Unit 1 Self-Introduction — 9
Unit 2 An Important Person or Thing — 17
Unit 3 Places — 25
Unit 4 Opinions — 33
Units 1–4 Review — 41
Unit 5 Biography — 43
Unit 6 Stories — 51
Unit 7 Solving Problems — 59
Unit 8 Final Presentation — 67
Units 5–8 Review — 75

A Guide to Vocal Warm-ups — 77
A Guide to Better Pronunciation — 78
A Guide to Writing a Better Presentation — 82
A Guide to Using Notes — 84
A Guide to Creating Super Slides — 86
A Guide to Class Warm-ups & Relaxation — 99
A Guide to Presentation Self-Reflections — 100

Scope and Sequence

Unit (Pages)	Theme	Share & Communicate	Watch the Model Presentation
Unit 1 (pp. 9–16)	Self-Introduction	■ Getting to know your classmates	My name is Mayu
Unit 2 (pp. 17–24)	An Important Person or Thing	■ Talking about people and things important to you	My Father
Unit 3 (pp. 25–32)	Places	■ Talking about interesting places	Angkor Wat
Unit 4 (pp. 33–40)	Opinions	■ Sharing opinions	Social Media
Units 1–4 Review (pp. 41–42)		■ Gestures review ■ Parts of a presentation ■ Introduction,	
Unit 5 (pp. 43–50)	Biography	■ Talking about people	Vincent van Gogh
Unit 6 (pp. 51–58)	Stories	■ Talking about your past experiences and stories	Life Lessons
Unit 7 (pp. 59–66)	Solving Problems	■ Expressing opinions about social and global issues	Plastic Pollution
Unit 8 (pp. 67–74)	Final Presentation	■ Expressing opinions ■ Talking about experiences ■ Talking about the future	Africa
Units 5–8 Review (pp. 75–76)		■ Transitions ■ Skills needed before, during, and after a	

Language to be Used	Plan & Write	Presentation Skills
- Greeting - Talking about family, school life, likes & dislikes, and experiences - Closing a presentation	- Writing an introduction, body, and conclusion	- Making good eye contact - Controlling your voice
- Telling the audience what you will talk about - Talking about an influential person and an important thing or idea - Asking questions - Sharing stories - Starting the conclusion	- Writing about something or someone important to you	- Using facial and hand gestures - Using the "Read, Look Up, Present" technique - Learning Dos and Don'ts while giving a presentation
- Describing places in a city - Giving reasons - Using slides	- Writing about and describing places	- Using slides and graphics - Using hand gestures
- Giving an opinion - Supporting and giving examples - Giving evidence - Asking the audience what they think	- Writing an opinion on a topic	- Speaking with emphasis - Using hand gestures for emphasis
body, and conclusion ■ Presentation dos and don'ts		
- Talking about a person's youth, life experiences, and accomplishments - Using transition words to describe life experiences	- Writing a biography	- Using hand gestures - Using gestures appropriately
- Setting up a story - Learning something from a story - Using common storytelling expressions	- Writing a personal story - Deciding what was learned from an experience	- Using gestures for storytelling - Speaking with emphasis
- Giving and supporting opinions - Giving examples and approximations - Stating facts - Showing increases and decreases	- Writing an opinion about an issue - Doing research	- Saying numbers - Using tables and graphs - Chunking sentences
—	- Choosing a theme for a presentation - Writing a great presentation	- Chunking - Reviewing gestures - Reviewing skills necessary before, during, and after a presentation
presentation ■ Gestures review		

Introduction

The ability to give a good presentation is a valuable 21st century skill. Here are the skills you gain when you become a good presenter:

- You develop confidence speaking in front of other people.
- You can express your opinions, ideas, and experiences.
- You become a better storyteller.
- By listening to presentations from your classmates, you broaden your point of view.
- You improve your planning and writing skills.
- Giving presentations in English helps you improve your English language skills.
- You will be able to communicate more deeply and effectively.

Using *Ready to Present*

Ready to Present will help you develop the necessary skills for becoming an effective presenter. Each unit in this book has several sections that are clear and easy to use.

Section	Description
Share & Communicate	This section is for communicative speaking with classmates. ▸ Talk about your experiences, thoughts, and feelings about the unit's theme.
Watch the Model Presentation	This section has both video and audio recordings of the model presentation. ▸ The model presentation introduces the unit's main theme.
Language to Be Used	This section has useful phrases and vocabulary that you can use for your presentations. ▸ Learn and practice natural phrases and expressions related to the unit's presentation topic.
Plan & Write	Plan and write your presentation using this section. ▸ Decide your topic, brainstorm your ideas, and make an outline. ▸ You will focus on the format of introduction, body, and conclusion. ▸ You will aim to use stories, opinions, facts and statistics, questions, and quotations throughout your presentations.
Presentation Skills	In this section, you will learn the basic skills for giving a good presentation. ▸ You will learn and improve skills such as eye contact, posture, voice control, speaking with emphasis, gestures, and others. ▸ You will also focus on the technique of "Read, Look Up, Present."

Guides to Better Presentations

These guides will help you further improve your presentation skills.

- A Guide to Vocal Warm-ups
- A Guide to Better Pronunciation
- A Guide to Writing a Better Presentation
- A Guide to Using Notes
- A Guide to Creating Super Slides
- A Guide to Class Warm-ups & Relaxation
- A Guide to Presentation Self-Reflections

Talking about Presentations in Your Life

Answer the questions below and then share your results with a partner.

1. In your life so far, how many presentations have you given?
   a. Less than 3.   b. Between 5–10.   c. More than 10.

2. Do you enjoy giving presentations?
   a. No, not at all.   b. Yes, kind of.   c. Yes, I really like giving a presentation.

3. Do you think you are good at giving presentations?
   a. No, I'm not good at giving presentations.
   b. I think I'm okay at giving presentations.
   c. I feel confident that I can give a good presentation.

4. Are you looking forward to taking this class?
   a. No, I don't like giving a presentation.
   b. Yes, I want to improve my presentation skills.
   c. Yes, definitely. I think this will be a great class.

5. Which of these skills do you find difficult?

Skill	I'm not good at this at all.	I'm okay with this skill.	I'm confident with this skill.
Making eye contact			
Using gestures			
Relaxing yourself			
Speaking loudly			
Memorizing a presentation			
Writing a presentation			

We hope that you find this book useful and stimulating. We want you to become a better presenter. With determination and hard work, you can make GREAT presentations.

The authors, Herman Bartelen and Malcolm Kostiuk

How to access the video and audio online

For activities with a camera icon (🎥) and/or a headset icon (🎧), the video and audio are available at the following website.

https://ngljapan.com/rtp-videoaudio/

You can access the video and audio as outlined below.
1. Visit the website above.
2. Click "Video (ビデオ)" or "Audio MP3 (音声ファイル)."
3. Click the link to the content you would like to watch or listen to.

Use the QR code to directly access the video and audio.

Unit 1

Self-Introduction

You will give your first presentation in class. This will be a self-introduction.

Share & Communicate

Use the questions to get to know your classmates. Talk about each question as long as you can.

Are you ...
... from Tokyo?
... into sports?

Do you ...
... have a big family?
... like J-pop music?
... enjoy cooking?

Have you ever ...
... traveled abroad?
... given a presentation in front of the whole class?

Did you ...
... wake up early this morning?
... make your own breakfast today?
... go to junior high school in this city?

Wh-questions
Who do you live with?
What is your favorite kind of movie?
Where did you grow up?
How did you get to school today?
How long have you studied English?

Watch the Model Presentation

Watch the presenter introduce herself to the class.

Hello everyone. My name is Mayu but my nickname is Maggie. Please call me Maggie.

First, let me begin by talking about my background and family. I was born in Yokote in Akita. I love the winter there because we can go skiing a lot. Anyway, I have a big family. I have two sisters, my parents, and a beautiful Shiba-inu called Snoopy. My father works in China now and my mother works part-time. My sisters are high school students. We all get along well.

Next, I'll talk about my school life. I'm an English major at school. I love all of my classes, especially my communication ones. At school, I also belong to the glee club because I love singing.

Finally, I'll tell you what I like to do in my free time. Well, I like to go out with my friends, watch movies, and surf the Internet. I also work part-time in a karaoke shop. I love food and so, I really enjoy cooking for my family. I especially like making curries.

So, now you know more about me. I hope you enjoyed my talk. I'm really looking forward to this presentation class. Thank you.

- background「生い立ち」 ■ work part-time「パートタイムで働く」 ■ get along well「仲が良い」
- major「専攻」 ■ belong to …「…に所属する」 ■ surf the Internet「インターネットでいろいろなサイトを見て回る」
- especially like「…を特に好む」 ■ look forward to …「…を楽しみに待つ」

 **Think!** What topics do you want to talk about in your self-introduction presentation? You must introduce **your background, family, school life, and free-time activities**.

Self-Introduction Unit 1

Language to Be Used

Below are phrases that you can use for your presentation. Try to use as many as possible.

Greeting	
Hello everyone.	
Good morning/afternoon/evening.	

Talking about family	
I have a small/big family.	**I have a big family**.
I have ___ sister(s) and ___ brother(s).	**I have** two **sisters and** one **brother**.
an only child	I'm **an only child**.

Talking about school life	
I major in …	**I major in** English.
My favorite subject is …	**My favorite subject is** science.
I especially love ___ class because …	**I especially love** history **class because** it is very interesting.
I belong to the ___ club.	**I belong to the** music **club**.

Talking about likes and dislikes	
I'm a big fan of …	**I'm a big fan of** anime.
I especially like …	**I especially like** cooking.
I'm very interested in …	**I'm very interested in** animation.
I like/really like/love …	**I love** studying.
I dislike/can't stand …	**I dislike** math class.

Talking about experiences	
When I was ___, …	**When I was** five, I lived in America.
In junior high school, …	**In junior high school**, I went to Australia for three weeks.

Using common expressions	
Well, …	**Well**, I like to go out with my friends and surf the Internet.
So, …	**So**, now you know more about me.
Anyway, …	**Anyway**, I have a big family.
because …	I love the winter there **because** we can go skiing a lot.

Closing a presentation
That's it for my self-introduction. I hope you enjoyed it.
Well, thank you for listening.

Plan & Write

A good presentation has three main parts: an introduction, a body, and a conclusion. Write your self-introduction below.

Introduction	
Greet the audience.	*Hello everyone.*
Say your name.	*My name is …*
Share one or two interesting things about your name or your background.	

Body	
Tell the audience what you will talk about.	*First, let me begin by talking about my background and family.*
Mention where you were born, grew up, and live now.	*I was born in …*
Introduce your family.	*I have a big/small family.* *I have ____ sisters/brothers. / I'm an only child.*

12

Body

Talk about your school life.

Next, I'll talk about my school life.
My favorite subject is …

Talk about what you like to do in your free time.

Finally, I'll tell you what I like to do in my free time.
Well, I like to …

I love …

I especially like …

Conclusion

Close your presentation and talk about how you feel.

So, that's it for me. I hope you enjoyed my talk. I'm really looking forward to this presentation class.

Thank the audience.

Thank you.

Presentation Skills — Eye Contact

It is very important to make good eye contact with your audience. Read the following points. Then, watch the video to see examples.

Do

- Look at everyone in the room.
- Look at all sides of the room.
- Look to the right, to the center, and to the left.

Look to the right.

Look to the center.

Look to the left.

Don't

- Don't look at the floor, ceiling, or desk most of the time.
- Don't look to the side or up, like you are memorizing.
- Don't look at only one or two people in the audience.

Pair Activity Practice reading the short sentences with a partner. Make good eye contact by looking straight ahead, right, and left.

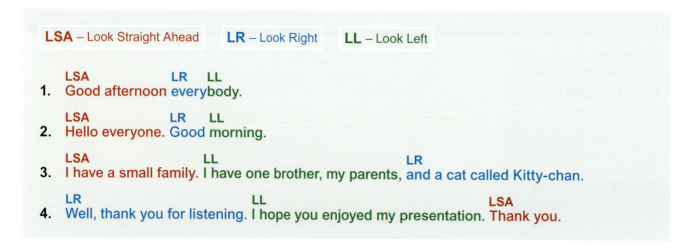

LSA – Look Straight Ahead   LR – Look Right   LL – Look Left

1. **LSA** Good afternoon **LR** every**LL**body.
2. **LSA** Hello everyone. **LR** Good **LL** morning.
3. **LSA** I have a small family. **LL** I have one brother, my parents, **LR** and a cat called Kitty-chan.
4. **LR** Well, thank you for listening. **LL** I hope you enjoyed my presentation. **LSA** Thank you.

Self-Introduction Unit 1

Presentation Skills › Voice Control

Your voice is an important tool when giving a presentation. Read the following points. Then, watch the video to see examples.

Do
- Speak LOUDLY.
- Speak CLEARLY.
- Speak at a good speed.

Don't
- Don't talk too slowly, or too quickly.
- Don't drop the volume at the end of a sentence.

 Work with a partner. Student A, use the instructions below. Student B, turn to the next page.

Student A

❶ Read this story to your partner. Use the Voice Control points above.

04

> First, let me tell you about my family and background. I was born in British Columbia in Canada. I especially like the summer there because we can go hiking in the mountains. Anyway, I have a big family. I have two older brothers, my parents, and a cat. Our cat's name is Tiger because he has black and orange stripes. My father is a businessman and my mother works part-time in a supermarket. My older brothers are university students.

❷ Listen to your partner's story. Fill in the blanks with the words you hear.

> Finally, I'll tell you what I like to do _____ _____ free time. Well, I like to go skateboarding, _____ video games, and go to the _____ with my _____. I especially like animation _____. I go skateboarding _____ _____ in the big park _____ my house. I _____ doing this with my friends. On _____, I usually watch movies and play video _____ by myself or with my family. It's also my day to _____ and go to bed _____.

15

Pair Activity Work with a partner. Student B, use the instructions below.

Student B

1 Listen to your partner's story. Fill in the blanks with the words you hear.

> First, let me tell you about my _____ and background. _____ _____ _____ in British Columbia in Canada. I especially like _____ _____ there because we can go hiking in the _____. Anyway, I have a _____ family. I have two older _____, my parents, and a _____. Our cat's name is Tiger because he has _____ and orange stripes. My father is a _____ and my mother works part-time in a _____. My older brothers are university _____.

2 Read this story to your partner. Use the Voice Control points on p. 15.

> Finally, I'll tell you what I like to do in my free time. Well, I like to go skateboarding, play video games, and go to the movies with my friends. I especially like animation films. I go skateboarding every weekend in the big park near my house. I love doing this with my friends. On Sundays, I usually watch movies and play video games by myself or with my family. It's also my day to relax and go to bed early.

Make a Great Presentation

Use your notes from the "Plan & Write" pages and give **a self-introduction presentation**. After your presentation, use the "Self-Reflections" at the back of the book. What can you improve?

Unit 2

An Important Person or Thing

You will give a presentation about an important person or thing in your life.

Share & Communicate

A What is important in your life now? Work with a partner and ask questions about the topics in the table. Use the phrases at the top of the table. Give reasons for your answers.

> How important are English studies in your life now?

> They're very important to me.

> Why's that?

> They're very important because I want to travel overseas one day and I think English is cool.

How important is (are) _____ in your life now?	It's (They're) not important at all.	It's (They're) not so important.	It's (They're) important to me.	It's (They're) very important.
English studies				✓
family				
fashion				
friends				
the Internet				
money				
music				
pets				
sports				
television				

B Ask a classmate the questions below to get ideas for your presentation.

1. Who is the most important person in your life now? Why?
2. What are two things in your life that you love? Why?

17

Watch the Model Presentation

Watch the presenter talk about an important person in his life.

Good afternoon.

Did you know that the first guitar was made more than 500 years ago in Europe? The first electric guitar was made in 1931. I know a lot about guitars because my father taught me. Today, I'm going to talk about my father, who had a big influence on my life. He showed me how to play guitar and he taught me to love music.

My father grew up in Kobe and moved to Tokyo when he was 10 years old. He got married to my mother after university. My father worked hard but he always found time to play guitar. He even played in a band. When I was in junior high school, my father bought me a guitar and taught me how to play. He encouraged me to listen to many kinds of music like jazz, rock, pop, and classical. Slowly, I became a better guitar player. Then, my father told me that I should join a band and I did this in high school.

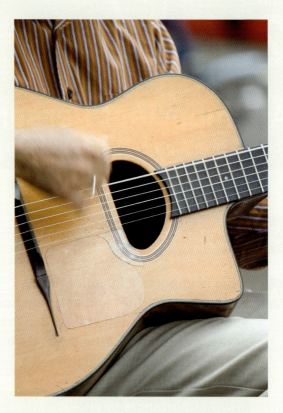

Next, I'd like to talk about my rock band, "The Orange Spoons." There are four members in our band, a singer, bass player, drummer, and me, the guitar player. We write our own songs and we are making an album now. When we had our first concert, my father came. I was so glad when he said that he liked our music.

So, in conclusion, my father has influenced my life in a big way because he taught me how to play guitar and love music. I really appreciate my father. Tower Records' logo is "No music, no life." My motto is "No father, no music!"

Thank you for listening.

- influence 「影響、…に影響を与える」 ■ grow up 「成長する」 ■ get married to … 「…と結婚する」
- encourage … to *do* 「…に~することを勧める」 ■ join a band 「バンドに入る」 ■ glad 「嬉しい」
- in a big way 「とても」 ■ appreciate 「…に感謝する」

 **Think!** What topic do you want to talk about? You must give a presentation about **a person or thing that is important in your life**.

An Important Person or Thing Unit 2

Language to Be Used

Below are some phrases that you can use for your presentation. Try to use as many as possible.

Telling the audience what you will talk about	
Today, I'm going to talk about …	**Today, I'm going to talk about** something that is very important to me.
I will talk about …	**I will talk about** someone who has influenced me a lot.
I will tell you about …	**I will tell you about** someone who has influenced me a lot.

Talking about an influential person	
He/She is important to me because …	**She is important to me because** she taught me English.
He/She influenced me by …	**He influenced me by** helping me learn to cook.

Talking about an important thing or idea	
I'm very interested in ___ because …	**I'm very interested in** traveling **because** we can learn so much.

Asking questions	
Did you know that …?	**Did you know that** the first guitar was made more than 500 years ago?
Who has …?	**Who has** influenced you the most?

Sharing stories	
I'd like to share a story that happened when …	**I'd like to share a story that happened when** I was in junior high school.
This is a story from when …	**This is a story from when** I was young.

Starting the conclusion	
In conclusion, …	**In conclusion,** my father has influenced my life in a big way.
To sum up, …	**To sum up,** my father has been a big influence.

Closing a presentation
Now you know something that is important to me. I hope you enjoyed my talk. Thank you.

Plan & Write

Use the information in "A Guide to Writing a Better Presentation" (p. 82) to plan and write your presentation.

1. Decide your topic.

   My Topic _____

2. Brainstorm.

3. Decide your main idea or point.

   Examples:
   - My father is important to me. He influenced me by helping me become a good guitar player.
   - An important thing in my life is my phone. I can't live without my phone.

4. Find stories, facts, and quotations, and write questions to use in your presentation.

5. Make an outline.

Introduction	
Greet the audience.	_____
Tell the audience what you will talk about.	_____
Say your main idea.	_____
Use a question, story, fact, or quotation.	_____

Body	
Talk about your main points.	_____

Body

Give details about the topic.

Give a reason for each of your opinions.

Use a question, story, fact, or quotation.

Conclusion

Give your final thoughts on the topic.

State your main idea again.

Thank the audience.

Presentation Skills | Facial & Hand Gestures

With a partner, read these important points about using gestures. Then, watch the video to see the examples.

1. Non-verbal communication makes your message powerful. It helps to express an idea or feeling.

2. Gestures help people remember what you say. If you put up three fingers to show the number "3", the audience both sees and hears the information. If your face looks worried when you say a sentence, the audience will clearly understand your feeling.

3. By learning basic gestures, you can express yourself more clearly in English.

Facial Gestures

Use your face to show your feelings. Read the example sentences and make the same gestures. Then, watch the video to see examples.

- If you are talking about something that is positive, show the feeling on your face.
- Show negative feelings for strong dislikes, embarrassment, or fear.

"I was extremely happy."

"I am a big fan of British music."

"I felt so embarrassed."

"And then someone yelled and I felt so scared."

"My test score was disappointing."

"I can't stand tomatoes."

Pair Activity: Say the following sentences out loud with your partner. Make a facial gesture that matches what the sentence is saying.

Positive
1. It was a very good day.
2. I learned how important it is to smile.
3. My homestay mother was a fantastic cook.
4. The countryside was beautiful.
5. I was very proud of my father.

Negative
1. I wasn't able to pass the test.
2. The food was terrible.
3. I was so tired, I couldn't move.
4. My face turned red. I was very embarrassed.
5. I fell and hurt my leg.

An Important Person or Thing Unit 2

Hand Gestures

Use hand gestures for emphasis. Watch the video to see examples.

1. Use two hands to emphasize basic points.

Put both hands out at the same time with your palms outstretched and facing up. This can be for positive, negative, or neutral statements.

2. Use your hands in a 1-2-3 pattern.

For example, you are going to say this sentence:
"There are several reasons why I feel that everyone should travel to a foreign country. First, we can learn about other cultures. Second, we can also learn about our own culture."

Put two hands out.
"There are several reasons why I feel that everyone should travel to a foreign country."

Put your right hand out.
"First, we can learn about other cultures."

Put your left hand out.
"Second, we can also learn about our own culture."

Class Activity Read the sentences below to practice the 1-2-3 pattern for hand gestures.

1. Hello everyone. Is music important to you? Personally, I cannot live without music.
2. Good morning. Today, many people don't read books. However, I think that we can learn so much from reading.
3. Who has influenced you the most in life? Your parents? A relative? Well, the most important person in my life was my high school teacher.
4. What did you do last night? As for me, I skateboarded for three hours. I can't live without skateboarding.
5. Good afternoon. It's a beautiful day, but today I'm going to talk about why I love rainy days.

Presentation Skills — Read, Look Up, Present

The "Read, Look Up, Present" technique is one that every good presenter uses.

- First, look down and read your notes or writing.
- Second, look up and connect with the audience.
- Third, say the line(s) you have memorized.

Practice the "Read, Look Up, Present" technique with the following sentences. Then, watch the video to see the examples.

1. Good morning everyone. Today, I'm going to talk about my sister. She has influenced me a lot in life.
2. My favorite kind of movie is horror because I like to be scared. Watching horror movies is never boring.
3. When I was 12 years old, I decided to drive my father's car. This was a big problem.
4. I love being with my friends. They help me when I'm down, and they laugh with me when I am happy. I can't live without my friends.

Presentation Skills — Dos and Don'ts While Giving a Presentation

There are things you should do and not do during your presentation to make it more powerful. Read the list below. Then, watch the video for more information and see examples.

Do
1. Take time to take a few deep breaths.
2. Use good posture.
3. Be sure to use gestures.
4. Remember to make good eye contact. Use the "Read, Look Up, Present" technique.
5. Remember to speak loudly and clearly.

Don't
1. Don't speak too quickly.
2. Don't lean on the podium.
3. Don't be stiff and motionless.
4. Don't only look straight ahead.
5. Don't speak too quietly.

Make a Great Presentation

Use your notes from the "Plan & Write" pages and give a presentation about **an important person or thing**. After your presentation, use the "Self-Reflections" at the back of the book. What can you improve?

Unit 3

Places
You will give a presentation about a place that you have been to or would like to visit.

Share & Communicate

Take turns asking a partner the questions below to get ideas for your presentation.

1. Would you rather have a vacation in the mountains or near the sea?
2. Would you rather take a vacation in Okinawa or Hokkaido?
3. Would you rather travel alone or with your family?
4. Would you rather visit a temple or go shopping?
5. Would you rather go zip lining or go to a zoo?
6. Where is your favorite place to hang out with your friends? Why?
7. Where is the most interesting place you have been to?
8. What place would you recommend that foreigners visit when they come to Japan?
9. What is your favorite city to visit?
10. Where was your favorite place to go to when you were younger?

Watch the Model Presentation

Watch the presenter talk about his trip to Angkor Wat.

Good afternoon everyone. There is a popular saying, "Once a year, go someplace you have never been before." I agree with this idea. Today, I will talk about Angkor Wat in Cambodia. I believe that Angkor Wat is one of the world's greatest buildings. First, I will explain about its history. And then, I will tell you about my first trip there.

Let's start with a short history of Angkor Wat. It is a Hindu temple that was built more than 900 years ago but now, it's Buddhist. It is the largest religious monument in the world and is a UNESCO World Heritage Site. Angkor Wat is an amazing temple, and it's a fantastic place to take photographs.

Now, I'll talk about my first trip there. Last year, my friends and I spent four days in Cambodia in the city of Siem Reap. We visited Angkor Wat and other temples. We visited Angkor Wat twice because there's so much to see. Angkor Wat has a moat and long wall around it so it takes a long time to see the whole area. There are many awesome statues and wall carvings to see. My friends and I spent two days taking photos, and we saw some incredible scenery. At the end of our trip, I realized how great Angkor Wat is.

I will never forget my trip. I was so impressed with the beauty of Angkor Wat. It is one of the world's greatest architectural wonders. I highly recommend that you go there. Through travel, we can learn about world history and discover beautiful places at the same time.

- saying「格言」 - Hindu temple「ヒンズー教の寺院」 - Buddhist「仏教(の)」 - religious monument「宗教的な遺跡」
- World Heritage Site「世界遺産」 - moat「堀」 - awesome「荘厳な、すばらしい」 - statue「像」
- wall carving「壁に彫り込まれた像」 - scenery「景色」 - realize「…を実感する」
- architectural wonder「感嘆すべき建築物」 - discover「…を発見する」

 **Think!** What topic do you want to talk about? You must give a presentation about **a place that is special to you**.

Places Unit 3

Language to Be Used

Below are phrases that you can use for your presentation. Try to use as many as possible.

Telling the audience what you will talk about

For my presentation today, I will talk about …	**For my presentation today, I will talk about** Kyoto.
First, I will explain about …	**First, I will explain about** Kyoto's history.
Second/Then, I will tell you about …	**Second, I will tell you about** the places you must see.

Describing places

There is a/an …	**There is a** big moat around the castle.
There are …	**There are** many statues.
It is known as …	**It is known as** the cultural capital of Japan.

Giving reasons

This place is special because …	**This place is special because** there are many temples.
The reason why I like this place is because …	**The reason why I like this place is because** my parents were born there.
I think it's a great place to visit because …	**I think it's a great place to visit because** there are many parks.
I feel it's a fantastic place to go because …	**I feel it's a fantastic place to go because** there are incredible skyscrapers.
I would rather …	**I would rather** have a vacation near the sea because I love swimming.
I prefer to …	**I prefer to** travel with my friends because they are a lot of fun.

Using slides

This photo was taken in …	**This photo was taken in** Cambodia.
This slide shows …	**This slide shows** a Buddhist statue.
The next slide is of …	**The next slide is of** Angkor Wat at sunset.
If you look at the bottom of the slide, you will see …	**If you look at the bottom of the slide, you will see** a deer.
On the right side, you can see …	**On the right side, you can see** two large skyscrapers.

Plan & Write

Use the information in "A Guide to Writing a Better Presentation" (p. 82) to plan and write your presentation.

1. Decide your topic.

    My Topic _____

2. Brainstorm.

3. Decide your main idea or point.

    Example:
    - Angkor Wat is one of the world's greatest buildings. My trip to Angkor Wat was one of my most memorable trips ever. If you go there, you will never forget it.

4. Find stories, facts, and quotations, and write questions to use in your presentation.

5. Make an outline.

Introduction		Slides to use
Greet the audience.		*Slide with title and my name.*
Tell the audience what you will talk about.		
Say your main idea.		
Use a question, story, fact, or quotation.		

Body		Slides to use
Talk about your main points.		

Body	Slides to use
Give details about the topic.	
Give a reason for each of your opinions.	
Use a question, story, fact, or quotation.	

Conclusion	Slides to use
Give your final thoughts on the topic.	
State your main idea again.	
Thank the audience.	

Presentation Skills › Slides & Graphics

Learn these important points to help you make a great graphic and give a good presentation with slides.

1. Use one number or statistic on a slide. Explain the number to the audience.

   Did you know that there are more than 1800 statues at Angkor Wat?

2. Write a famous quote on your slide. Connect it to your topic.

   Look at this popular quote about traveling. I definitely agree.

3. Use one strong image that connects to your topic and fill the whole screen with it. For example, if you are presenting about Angkor Wat, use an image of the temple.

   I believe that Angkor Wat is one of the world's greatest buildings.

4. Use complimentary colors to make your visuals more effective.

   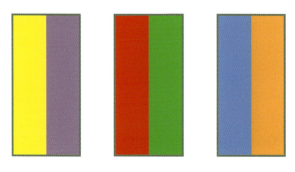

5. Use black on white or white on black. These are powerful and simple combinations.

   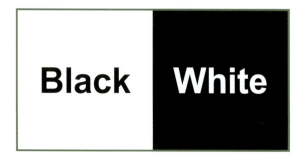

6. DON'T do the following:
   - Don't look at the slide or graphic while you are speaking.
   - Don't turn your back to the audience.
   - Don't stand in front of the slide or graphic and block it from the audience.
   - Don't read from the slide or graphic.

Places Unit 3

Presentation Skills — Hand Gestures 2

Below are more gestures good presenters use. Watch the video to see examples.

1. Raise one or two fists to show that you feel strongly about an issue or thing.

"I think it's important to always do your best!"

"We must do something soon, or it will be too late."

2. Put one or two hands on your heart or upper chest to show an emotion or feeling. It can be positive or negative.

"Personally, I love my hometown."

"It was a very difficult time."

3. Use one or two outstretched hands, palms facing up, to grab the audience's attention.

"How do YOU feel about this topic?"

"Do you think we can make the world a better place?"

4. Use your fingers to indicate order or numbers.

"There is one main reason why I went there."
"The first important thing is to make strong eye contact."

"There are two people who have influenced me a lot."
"The second important point is to speak loudly and clearly."

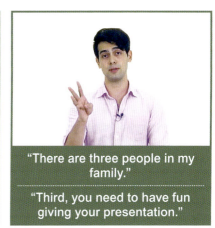
"There are three people in my family."
"Third, you need to have fun giving your presentation."

| Pair Activity | Say the following sentences out loud with your partner. Make a hand gesture that matches what the sentence is saying. Watch the video to see the answers. |

1. First of all, I learned how important it is to smile. Second, I learned that we must be positive.

2. I loved my high school.

3. There are two reasons why I decided to study English. First, it is a common world language. Second, English is important for the global economy.

4. Personally, I'm not a big fan of horror movies.

5. How do YOU feel about this topic?

6. As for me, I learned so much from my homestay in New Zealand.

7. I think it's important that more homes have solar power panels.

8. What does everyone in the audience think about this question?

9. If you want to be a good guitar player, there are several things you have to do. First of all, you have to know how to tune a guitar. Second, you have to know how to play chords. Third, you need to practice a lot.

10. I strongly feel that everyone should study history.

11. We all should be careful about how we spend money.

12. My sister and I are best friends.

Make a Great Presentation

Use your notes from the "Plan & Write" pages and give a presentation about **a place that is special to you.** After your presentation, use the "Self-Reflections" at the back of the book. What can you improve?

Unit 4

Opinions

You will give an opinion on an issue.

Share & Communicate

Ask your partner what she or he thinks about the topics below. Use the questions and opinion phrases.

Questions	Opinion phrases	Topics
What do you think of …?	I think that …	- space travel
How do you feel about …?	I don't think that …	- Japanese TV
Why?	I feel that …	- Kyoto
Why's that?	I don't feel that …	- playing video games
	In my opinion, …	- robots
		- homework
		- this school
		- traveling overseas
		- using social media
		- your neighborhood

What do you think of space travel?

I think that it would be exciting. I would love to travel in space.

Really? Why?

Well, it would be cool to see the earth from space.

Watch the Model Presentation

Watch the presenter give her opinion about social media.

Hi everyone. I have a question for you. How many of you have a Facebook account? Okay ... how many have Twitter or LINE? As you can see, many of us use social media—or SNS. But how much does it benefit our lives? Even though I use Facebook and LINE every day, I strongly believe that social media can be harmful. Today, I want to tell you the two reasons why I feel this way.

First of all, social media takes up too much of our time. I read in an article that an average student spends 90 minutes a day on social media. That is 15 hours a week. Almost the same as my part-time job! Personally, I think that time should be spent on a hobby or having fun with friends or family. To me, 15 hours a week reading other people's comments and watching viral videos does not give you a better life.

Another way that social media is harmful is that it can be dangerous. When you meet new people online, you don't know who they really are. It is easy for a stranger to lie about his or her profile. At the same time, there is a lot of online bullying and cyberstalking. This is a growing trend. So, I truly believe that social media can be harmful.

Social media can be enjoyable if you use it correctly. But in my opinion, spending too much time online can definitely be harmful. How do you feel about social media?

- benefit 「…の利益になる」　- harmful 「有害な」　- article 「記事」　- average 「平均的な」　- viral video 「口コミ動画」
- stranger 「見知らぬ人」　- lie 「嘘をつく」　- profile 「プロフィール」　- bullying 「(弱い者)いじめ」
- cyberstalking 「サイバーストーキング（SNSをはじめとしたインターネットを使って行うストーキングやハラスメント）」
- spend time online 「インターネットをして時間を過ごす」

 **Think!**　What topic do you want to talk about? You must give a presentation about **an issue** that is important to you.

Opinions Unit 4

Language to Be Used

Below are phrases that you can use for your presentation. Try to use as many as possible.

Giving an opinion	
Personally, I think that …	**Personally, I think that** children should learn at least two languages.
I don't think that …	**I don't think that** children should learn more than one language in elementary school.
I feel that …	**I feel that** people should be able to speak at least two languages.
I don't feel that …	**I don't feel that** children should learn two languages in elementary school.
In my opinion, …	**In my opinion,** all children should study at least two languages.
To me, …	**To me,** knowing at least two languages is best.

Supporting and giving examples	
I feel this way because …	I think that people should use their phones less. **I feel this way because** it's too easy for us to be controlled by our phones.
The reason why I think this way is because …	**The reason why I think this way is because** many people check their phones all the time.
One example is …	**One example is** my friend Julie, who checks her phone every five minutes.
Another example is …	**Another example is** when people sleep with their phones beside them.
In fact, …	**In fact,** there are now more phones than people in the world.
In addition, …	**In addition,** there are people who would cry if you took away their phones.

Giving evidence	
I read …	**I read** on the WWF website that polar bears are an endangered species.
According to …,	**According to** the WWF, polar bears need to be protected.

Asking the audience what they think	
What do you think of/about …?	**What do you think of** space travel?
How do you feel about …?	**How do you feel about** social media?
What's your opinion of/about …?	**What's your opinion about** this school?

Plan & Write

Use the information in "A Guide to Writing a Better Presentation" (p. 82) to plan and write your presentation.

1. Decide your topic.

   My Topic _____

2. Brainstorm.

3. Decide your main idea or point.

   Example:
   - Social media can be harmful. People spend too much time online and it can be dangerous because of bullying and cyberstalking.

4. Find stories, facts, and quotations, and write questions to use in your presentation.

5. Make an outline.

Introduction	
Greet the audience.	
Tell the audience what you will talk about.	
Say your main idea.	
Use a question, story, fact, or quotation.	

Body	
Talk about your main points.	

Opinions | Unit 4

Body

Give details about the topic.

Give a reason for each of your opinions.

Use a question, story, fact, or quotation.

Conclusion

Give your final thoughts on the topic.

State your main idea again.

Thank the audience.

Presentation Skills > Emphasizing Words with Gestures

There are different ways to emphasize key words or points in your presentation.

1. Say a word louder.
2. Say certain words or expressions slowly.
3. Use a simple hand gesture to emphasize your main points.

Activity 1

A Read the sentences below and say the expressions in bold louder and slowly for emphasis.

1. Personally, **I think** it's **important** to know all the facts.
2. **Don't you think** that there are too many people in this world?
3. **I feel** that it's **important** to have **good** presentation skills.
4. **Did you know** that most people fall in love **only once**?
5. **I feel** that we **must** communicate about the problem first.
6. In **my opinion**, it's important to know at least **two** languages.
7. How do **you feel** about this situation?
8. **According** to the WWF, elephants **need to be protected**.
9. **How** do you **feel** about **religion**?
10. What do **you think** about space travel?

B Repeat the sentences above. Use a simple two-handed gesture at the beginning of the sentence and keep your hands outstretched. Look at the picture.

C Now, watch the video for examples.

Opinions   Unit 4

Activity 2

The words below are often spoken with emphasis.

and	more	a lot
however	most	not
but	too	no

A Read the sentences below and say the words in bold louder and slowly for emphasis.

1. I think children should learn two languages **and** spend at least one semester abroad in high school.
2. I see your point; **however**, I still believe smoking should be banned in public spaces.
3. It is important to enjoy eating **but** we shouldn't waste food.
4. **Most** people are against smoking in public.
5. There is **a lot** we can do concerning plastic pollution.
6. Some students spend **too** much time playing video games.
7. I believe that all students should **not** use their phones in class.
8. There are **no** good reasons to allow phones in class.
9. The best thing is to put in **more** effort.
10. I would like to go to Mars **but** I would **not** want to travel in a rocket.

B Repeat the sentences above. Use a right-hand, left-hand gesture. The right hand should be stretched out for the first part of the sentence and then the left hand will be stretched out for the second half of the sentence. Of course, you can switch hands. Look at the pictures.

C Now, watch the video for examples.

Activity 3

Read the presentation below out loud with a partner. Say the words in **bold** and **CAPITAL LETTERS** with more emphasis and feeling. When there are spaces between the words, use a longer pause.

WATER is **VERY** **IMPORTANT** in our lives. **HOWEVER**, there are **MANY PROBLEMS** concerning water. For this presentation, I will first share some **SURPRISING** facts about water. Then, I will talk about some simple things that **WE** can do to **PROTECT** **WATER**.

3-SECOND PAUSE

FIRST, here are some **SHOCKING** facts. Today, more than **1.5** **BILLION PEOPLE** do **NOT** have clean water. In addition, did **YOU** **KNOW** that **HALF** of the world's schools do **NOT** have clean water? Finally, **70%** of the world's water is used for agriculture but **MUCH OF IT** is **WASTED**. These statistics show us that the world has **SERIOUS** water problems.

3-SECOND PAUSE

NOW, I will share some simple things **WE** can do to save water. **FIRST**, it's **VERY IMPORTANT** to use **LESS** water. Turn **OFF** the water while you brush your teeth, or wash your hands or body. **SECOND**, drink **MORE** tap water and **NOT** from plastic bottles because we waste water when we make bottled water. **FINALLY**, use **LESS** electricity because electricity uses a **LOT** of water. These are only a **FEW STATISTICS** that show us the **PROBLEMS** with water.

3-SECOND PAUSE

In summary, **WATER** is one of the world's **MOST IMPORTANT** resources **AND** we need to **PROTECT** it **MORE**. I **STRONGLY** **BELIEVE** we need to think **MORE DEEPLY** about how to improve our use of the **WORLD'S** **WATER**.

Make a Great Presentation

Use your notes from the "Plan & Write" pages and give a presentation about **an issue that is important to you**. After your presentation, use the "Self-Reflections" at the back of the book. What can you improve?

Units 1–4 Review

A Match the statements (1–7) with the correct gestures (a–g).

1. I can't stand insects.
2. First, I decided to get a part-time job. Second, I saved all the money I made.
3. I was happy to hear this.
4. I love my hometown.
5. What do YOU want to do with your life?
6. The second important thing is to create a schedule for your studies.
7. I was sad to hear this story.

B Match the parts of a presentation (1–7) with the items (a–l). The first one has been done for you.

1. Introduction/Greeting
2. Common expressions
3. Closing
4. Telling the audience the main idea
5. Concluding a presentation
6. Giving reasons
7. Using slides

a. **1** Hello.
b. ☐ This place is special to me because I grew up here.
c. ☐ On the right side, you can see the mountains.
d. ☐ Thank you for listening.
e. ☐ Today, I will talk about someone that is important to me: my sister.
f. ☐ Anyway,
g. ☐ In conclusion, I want to say that I truly appreciate my father.
h. ☐ Thank you.
i. ☐ Well, …
j. ☐ In my opinion, everyone should learn two languages.
k. ☐ I hope you enjoyed my presentation.
l. ☐ Good afternoon everyone.

C All outlines and writing should have an introduction, body, and conclusion. Read the sentences and write down whether they are from the introduction, body, or conclusion.

1. _____ The presenter gives the main idea or theme of the presentation.
2. _____ The presenter thanks the audience.
3. _____ The presenter greets the audience.
4. _____ The presenter talks about the main points of the presentation.
5. _____ The presenter gives final thoughts on the topic.
6. _____ The presenter gives reasons for opinions.
7. _____ The presenter repeats the main idea of the presentation.

D The sentences below describe good and bad presentation actions. Circle "Do" or "Don't" to complete the sentences.

1. **Do/Don't** use facial gestures to show positive and negative feelings.
2. **Do/Don't** use one number or statistic on a slide.
3. **Do/Don't** talk too quietly or slowly.
4. **Do/Don't** look down at the floor most of the time.
5. **Do/Don't** turn your back to the audience.
6. **Do/Don't** emphasize key words by saying them louder.
7. **Do/Don't** speak loudly and clearly.
8. **Do/Don't** look at all sides of the room and everyone in it.
9. **Do/Don't** drop the volume at the end of a sentence.
10. **Do/Don't** use your hands to emphasize basic points.

Unit 5

Biography

You will give a presentation about a person and his or her life.

Share & Communicate

A In a group or with a partner, use the questions for discussion.

1. Name 5 famous Japanese people who have died.
2. Name 5 famous foreign people who have died.
3. You can have dinner with one famous person from the past. Who would you choose? Why?
4. You can have dinner with any two people. Who would you choose? Why?

B Interview a partner about his or her life. Use the questions below.

1. When and where were you born?
2. Where did you grow up?
3. What is a good memory from your childhood?
4. What did you like about elementary school? What didn't you like?
5. What did you like about junior high school and high school? What didn't you like?
6. What or who influenced you a lot as you were growing up?

Watch the Model Presentation

Watch the presenter talk about Vincent van Gogh.

I love painting, and one of my favorite artists is the Dutch painter, Vincent van Gogh. Unfortunately, Van Gogh had an unhappy life and killed himself at 37 years old. Today, I'm going to talk about his life and work, and tell you why I love his art.

Vincent van Gogh was born in the Netherlands in 1853. He began painting when he was 28 years old. Later, Vincent moved to Paris where he studied art. From 1888 to 1890, Van Gogh lived in southern France. Here, his paintings became very colorful and emotional. However, Van Gogh couldn't sell any of his paintings and he was poor.

Vincent van Gogh had an unhappy life. He had two sad romances but did not marry. He had mental problems that slowly became worse. He spent his last year in a hospital and finally, in 1890, he shot himself and died. After his death, Van Gogh's greatest works were all sold in less than three years. Today, Van Gogh is considered one of the greatest artists of all time.

Now I would like to tell you three reasons why I admire him. First, he devoted his life to art and created more than 900 paintings, even though many people didn't like his work. The second reason is that his paintings are so passionate and emotional. Finally, I love the fantastic, bright colors in his art. My favorite painting is "Starry Night." It is a magical painting of the night sky over a town.

Although Vincent van Gogh only sold one painting during his life, today his art is famous throughout the world. Unfortunately, he lived a sad life but still, he gave the world such inspirational art. Thank you Vincent van Gogh. You are a beautiful person!

- unfortunately「残念ながら」 ■ the Netherlands「オランダ」 ■ emotional「情緒的な」
- mental problem「精神機能障害」 ■ shoot oneself「銃で自殺する」 ■ in less than three years「3年も経たずに」
- be considered ...「…と見なされる」 ■ admire「…を称賛する」 ■ devote「…を捧げる」 ■ passionate「情熱的な」
- magical「魅惑的な」 ■ still「それでも」 ■ inspirational「感情を揺さぶる(ような)」

 **Think!** What topic do you want to talk about? You must give a presentation about **a person that you admire or who has influenced you**.

Biography Unit 5

Language to Be Used

Below are phrases that you can use for your presentation. Try to use as many as possible.

Talking about a person's youth	
He/She was born in …	**He was born in** the Netherlands in 1853.
When he/she was young, …	**When he was young,** Van Gogh wasn't very successful.
As a young boy/girl, …	**As a young boy,** he loved traveling.

Talking about life experiences	
From ___ to ___, …	**From** 1888 **to** 1890, Van Gogh lived in southern France.
In ___, …	**In** 1878, he decided to live in Belgium.
work as …	He **worked as** a school teacher.
When he/she was …	**When he was** 28 years old, he moved to Paris.
He/She moved to ___ where he/she …	**He moved to** Paris **where he** studied art.
He/She decided to …	**He decided to** become a painter.
In the end, …	**In the end,** he moved to southern France.
Finally, …	**Finally,** he decided to return to Paris.

Talking about a person's accomplishments	
One reason why I admire him/her …	**One reason why I admire him** is that he worked hard.
There are three reasons why …	**There are three reasons why** I admire him.
First, …	**First,** he spent every day thinking about art.
The second reason is that …	**The second reason is that** he painted with such emotion.
Finally, …	**Finally,** I love the bright colors in his works.
become well-known for …	He **became well-known for** his paintings of sunflowers.

Using transition words to describe life experiences	
Unfortunately, …	**Unfortunately,** he lived a sad life.
However, …	**However,** Van Gogh couldn't sell any of his paintings.
While …	**While** he lived in England, he was a school teacher.
Instead, …	**Instead,** he traveled around Belgium.
For example, …	**For example,** he painted every day.
Today, …	**Today,** he is famous around the world.
Although …	**Although** many people didn't like his work, he continued painting.
even though …	He continued painting, **even though** many people didn't like his work.

Plan & Write

Use the information in "A Guide to Writing a Better Presentation" (p. 82) to plan and write your presentation. Also, see "A Guide to Creating Super Slides" (p. 86) to create great slides.

1. Decide your topic.

   My Topic _____

2. Brainstorm.

3. Decide your main idea or point.

   Example:
   - I love the paintings of Vincent van Gogh. He lived a sad life, but his paintings inspired many people like me.

4. Find stories, facts, and quotations, and write questions to use in your presentation.

5. Make an outline.

Introduction		Slides to use
Greet the audience.		Slide with title and my name.
Tell the audience what you will talk about.		
Say your main idea.		
Use a question, story, fact, or quotation.		

Body		Slides to use
Talk about your main points.		

Biography Unit 5

Body		Slides to use
Give details about the topic.		
Give a reason for each of your opinions.		
Use a question, story, fact, or quotation.		

Conclusion		Slides to use
Give your final thoughts on the topic.		
State your main idea again.		
Thank the audience.		

47

Presentation Skills Hand Gestures 3

Gestures are an important part of English presentations. In this activity, you will learn various gestures. Use them to make your message clearer and more powerful.

Activity

A With a partner, match the statements (1–9) with the gestures in the pictures (a–i). Then, watch the video to see the answers.

1. It was a very small part of the work.
2. I didn't understand.
3. I was really hoping to get the job.
4. First, I will tell you about her family.
5. The costs for his business went higher.
6. On the one hand, he lived a sad life. On the other hand, he created great art.
7. The young boy was very short.
8. Now listen to my story.
9. Everything was okay in the end.

B With a partner, match the statements (1–9) with the gestures in the pictures (a–i). Then, watch the video to see the answers.

1. I didn't like it and I told the children to stop.
2. I forgot my keys. I felt so stupid!
3. What do YOU really want from life?
4. The prices went down!
5. I didn't understand what he was saying.
6. It was quite long.
7. It was no good!
8. I was very surprised to hear the story.
9. I really believe that we all can do it.

Tips for Using Gestures

With a partner, read these tips about using gestures. Then, watch the video to see examples.

1. There is an appropriate area for gestures. It is from the shoulder area to the waist. If you go outside of the area, it will be distracting.

2. Don't be too extreme with your gestures. Look at the pictures below.

3. Practice your gestures at the same time you rehearse your presentation. Plan which gestures you will use.
4. Make sure your hand gestures and facial gestures match what you are saying.
5. Make your hand gestures as smooth as possible.
6. Don't use rude gestures.

Make a Great Presentation

Use your notes from the "Plan & Write" pages and give a presentation about **a person you admire or who has influenced you**. After your presentation, use the "Self-Reflections" at the back of the book. What can you improve?

Unit 6

Stories

You will share stories and experiences from your life.

Have you ever lost anything valuable?

Yes, I lost an expensive watch when I was in high school.

How did that happen?

I forgot my bag on the train. I had put my watch in my bag. It was a gift from my grandfather.

Did you ever find it?

Share & Communicate

Discuss the questions below to share stories and experiences from your life.

1. Have you ever lost anything valuable?
2. Have you ever found money or something valuable?
3. Have you ever had something stolen from you?
4. Have you ever won something?
5. Have you ever gotten really angry at someone?
6. Have you ever had a bad travel experience?
7. Have you had any interesting travel experiences abroad?
8. Have you ever had an embarrassing incident at school, at home, or at work?
9. Have you ever gotten lost?
10. Have you ever been really sick or stayed in a hospital?

Watch the Model Presentation

Watch the presenter talk about a lesson he learned in life.

Good afternoon everyone. Have you ever made a big mistake in your life? Well, I have. Today, I would like to tell you about a bad experience that taught me an important lesson.

Last year, I really wanted to spend the summer backpacking through Europe. Because the trip was expensive, I decided to work two part-time jobs. First, I got a job at a convenience store on weekends. Then, I started the second job teaching at a cram school three nights a week. I was working almost 30 hours a week!

Working part-time AND attending school were pretty difficult. Every morning I left my house at 6 a.m. I went to school during the day, and then I rushed to my part-time job at night. My schedule was extremely tiring, but after three months, I saved enough to buy my ticket for Europe.

But then disaster struck. Just before my final exams in July, I got really sick and I missed many classes. I was so sick that it was impossible to study or work. In the end, I failed three classes and had to spend the summer at school. I was in shock. My teachers were in shock. My parents were in shock. I could not spend my summer in Europe!

What did I learn from this terrible experience? I learned that it is very important to plan carefully for your goals and to keep a balance in life between work, school, and relaxation. In fact, I'm planning for my next European vacation now. This time, I will be successful!

- make a mistake「間違いを犯す」 ■ lesson「教訓」 ■ backpack「リュック1つで旅をする」 ■ cram school「塾」
- rush to …「…に大急ぎで行く」 ■ extremely「極端に」 ■ tiring「きつい」 ■ save「貯金する」
- disaster「災難」 ■ strike「襲う」 ■ fail a class「単位を落とす」 ■ in shock「ショックを受けていて」
- terrible「ひどい」 ■ plan「計画する」 ■ carefully「慎重に」 ■ goal「目標」 ■ keep a balance「バランスを保つ」

Think! What story do you want to talk about? You can talk about **your own story or someone else's story**. You must tell a story from which you learned something.

Language to Be Used

Below are phrases that you can use for your presentation. Try to use as many as possible.

Setting up the story	
Have you ever …?	**Have you ever** made a big mistake in your life?
I would like to tell you …	**I would like to tell you** about something that happened to me last year.
I was + verb-ing	**I was working** almost 30 hours a week.
I used to …	**I used to** belong to the baseball club.

Learning something from a story	
Even though …	**Even though** it wasn't a good experience, it taught me an important lesson.
I learned that …	**I learned that** it is very important to plan carefully for your goals.
In the future, I will …	**In the future, I will** be smarter with my plans.
I realized that …	**I realized that** I was working too much.

Using common storytelling expressions	
Last year, …	**Last year,** I wanted to spend the summer backpacking through Europe.
First, …	**First,** I got a job at a convenience store.
Then …	**Then** I started the second job at a cram school.
As soon as …	**As soon as** my classes finished, I rushed to the cram school.
In the end, …	**In the end,** I failed three classes.
So, …	**So,** I decided to cancel my trip.
Anyway, …	**Anyway,** there were many things to do.
However, …	**However,** my family was not happy with me.
The next day, …	**The next day,** I went to my part-time job and quit.
But then, …	**But then,** I began to think about the money I could get.
One day, …	**One day,** I fell asleep during class.
Before …	**Before** I went, I worked two part-time jobs.
After …	**After** I finished summer school, I started to save money again.
When …	**When** I returned to work, I was more careful.

Plan & Write

Use the information in "A Guide to Writing a Better Presentation" (p. 82) to plan and write your presentation.

1. Decide your topic.

   My Topic _____

2. Brainstorm.

3. Decide your main idea or point.

   Example:
   - I had a bad experience while working two part-time jobs and going to school. I learned that it is important to keep a balance in life between work, school, and relaxation.

4. Find stories, facts, and quotations, and write questions to use in your presentation.

5. Make an outline.

Introduction	
Greet the audience.	
Tell the audience what you will talk about.	
Use a question, fact, or quotation.	

Body	
Introduce your story.	

Body

Tell your story and give details.

Say how you felt in the end.

Conclusion

Give your final thoughts on the story.

Say what you learned.

Thank the audience.

Presentation Skills › Gestures for Storytelling

There are gestures you can use to make the telling of a story more powerful.

Activity

With a partner, match the statements (1–9) with the gestures in the pictures (a–i). Then, watch the video to see the answers.

1. It costs a lot of money if you want to travel around the world.
2. We made it to the top.
3. This is important!
4. The trip was great!
5. I was so angry!
6. First I went to London, and then I went to Paris.
7. It was very boring.
8. I cried out, "Watch out!"
9. I was so cold.

Presentation Skills — Speaking with Emphasis

The adverbs below are useful for emphasizing ideas or words.

> very   definitely   extremely   so   quite   too   really

Activity

A Say the following sentences out loud and emphasize the adverbs in **bold**.

1. I was **very** surprised when the door opened.
2. On our trip through South America, we will **definitely** visit Peru.
3. The pyramids are **extremely** old.
4. The tour guide was **so** excited as we got closer to Mt. Fuji.
5. The temple was **quite** beautiful.
6. It wasn't **too** difficult to swim across the river.
7. I was **really** impressed with the view of the lake.

B Say the sentences below and emphasize the words in **bold**. Use a two-hand gesture, or a right-hand, left-hand gesture. When you are finished, watch the video to see examples.

1. (two-hand gesture) The problem is **quite** serious.
2. (right-hand, left-hand gesture) They told us that the boat was **too** old to use.
3. (right-hand, left-hand gesture) During our trip to Europe, we had a **really** good time.
4. (right-hand, left-hand gesture) The weather in India in summertime is **extremely** hot.
5. (two-hand gesture) I was **very** happy to see my friends and family again.
6. (two-hand gesture) Next time, we will **definitely** bring a sleeping bag.
7. (right-hand, left-hand gesture) We were **so** excited to see the top of Mt. Fuji.

C Speaking slowly and emphasizing words are two ways to focus on points in your presentation. Practice with the passages below. Say the words in **bold** louder and with more feeling. When there are spaces between the words, use a longer pause.

1. I'd like to tell you one of my **funny** train   stories.   **One day**, in the morning,   I was waiting for the **train** to go to **school**.   My **hair** was in a ponytail on that day.   The train was **extremely crowded** when I got in.   The door closed   **but then**,   I felt **strange**.   My head **couldn't** move.   I **realized** that my ponytail was **stuck** in the door   and I **couldn't do   anything**.   I was **scared** because I **wasn't** able to **move**. **Luckily**,   the door **opened** at the **next** station   and my hair was released.   **Whew**!   I was **scared** when this happened but **now**   it is a **funny** train story for me.

2. I'd like to share one of my **funny** stories.   **One day**,   my **friend** asked me to **go shopping** with her at a **furniture** store.   **After** we **finished**,   we **went** to the **massage chair** section in the store.   There was an **extremely expensive** chair that cost **600,000 yen**   and I   wanted to **try it**.   I sat down in the chair   **but** it **didn't move**.   **So**,   I **took** the remote control and **pushed** the **speed** button.   **Nothing**   moved.   I **kept increasing** the speed and pressure   but the chair **still   didn't   move**.   Finally,   I **gave up**. I was walking away when I **noticed** an **older** man sitting in the chair   next to mine. He was **sleeping**   but his **massage** chair   was **shaking**   a lot.   I **realized** that the **remote control** that **I** was using was the **controller** for **his** chair. I felt **embarrassed** but later   my **friend** and I   **laughed   so   much**.

Make a Great Presentation

Use your notes from the "Plan & Write" pages and give a presentation about **your own story or someone else's story**. After your presentation, use the "Self-Reflections" at the back of the book. What can you improve?

Unit 7

Solving Problems
You will give a presentation about social and global issues.

Share & Communicate

A Use the phrases at the top of the table and take the survey with a partner. Then, share your results with another classmate.

What are your feelings about the issue of _____?	I don't think this is a serious issue in Japan.	I don't know very much about this topic.	I know a little about this, and I want to learn more.	I think this is a serious problem in Japan. I want to help change it.
bullying				
care for the elderly				
food waste				
legal voting age				
nomophobia				
nuclear power				
plastic waste				
polluted beaches				
women's equality				
youth crime				

B Ask a classmate the questions below to get ideas for your presentation.

1. Are you interested in social or global issues? Why or why not?
2. Do you read or watch TV programs about social or global issues?
3. How do you get your news? From TV, magazines, or the Internet?
4. What do you think are some of the serious social problems in Japan right now?
5. What do you think are some of the serious problems in the world right now?

Watch the Model Presentation

Watch the presenter talk about the problem with plastic.

Our planet is sick. The ice is melting in the North and South Poles. There are rising sea levels around the world, and the coral reefs are dying in Australia. These are really big environmental problems. I'm sure many of us don't know what to do to help. But there is an environmental issue that we can all help to change. What is it? Plastic pollution. Plastic is used in almost everything we use: grocery bags, PET bottles, and even the chairs you are sitting on.

Did you know that 38 billion water bottles are wasted every year, and about 10% of all plastic in the world ends up in the oceans? This plastic is a danger to fish, whales, and seabirds. They eat this plastic and it fills their stomachs. Eventually they die from starvation. This is a really big problem! Today, I want to tell you what we can do to solve the problem of plastic pollution.

First, everyone needs to reduce the amount of plastic they use. Stop buying bottled water and carry a reusable bottle with you. When it is empty, fill it up from the nearest water tap in your school. Also, you don't need to use straws for your drinks. These are a waste. Instead, just drink directly from your cup or glass. Next, never use plastic grocery bags when you go to the supermarket. Bring reusable cloth bags to take your food home in. Finally, always try to follow the 3Rs of Reduce, Reuse, and Recycle.

Our planet has many environmental problems but we can all do something about plastic pollution. Let's start today! If we all use less plastic in our lives, we can help protect the environment.

- planet「惑星」
- melt「溶ける」
- North (South) Pole「北(南)極」
- rising「上昇する」
- sea level「海水面、海水位」
- coral reef「サンゴ礁」
- environmental problem/issue「環境問題」
- pollution「汚染」
- grocery bag「買い物袋」
- billion「10億」
- end up in …「最後に…に行く」
- eventually「最終的に」
- die from starvation「餓死する」
- solve「…を解決する」
- reduce「…を減らす」
- amount「量」
- reusable「再利用できる」
- empty「空っぽの」
- water tap「給水栓、水道」
- straw「ストロー」
- waste「廃棄物、ごみ」
- take … home in「…を家に持って行く」

Think! What issue do you want to talk about? You must give a presentation about **a social or global issue that you are interested in**.

Solving Problems Unit 7

Language to Be Used

Below are phrases that you can use for your presentation. Try to use as many as possible.

Giving opinions	
Personally, I think/don't think …	**Personally, I think** that we shouldn't have school uniforms.
I feel/don't feel that …	**I feel that** 18-year olds should not be able to vote.
In my opinion, …	**In my opinion,** English education should be improved.
As far as I'm concerned, …	**As far as I'm concerned,** living alone is a valuable experience.

Supporting opinions	
I think/feel this way because …	**I think this way because** students should be able to choose what they want to study.
The reason why I think so is because …	**The reason why I think so is because** of my research.
Another reason is that …	**Another reason is that** I feel students should have more freedom.
Finally, …	**Finally,** I think it's important for students to make their own choices.

Giving examples	
One example is …	**One example is** when students can't stop checking their phones.
For instance, …	**For instance,** some students go to bed with their phones.
For example, …	**For example,** some students go to sleep with their phones beside them.

Giving approximations	
About …	**About** 20% of the students have part-time jobs.
Around …	**Around** 30 million foreigners visited Japan last year.
Approximately …	**Approximately** 75 teachers work at this school.
Almost …	**Almost** 50,000 penguins were rescued.

Stating facts	
In fact, …	**In fact,** more people are addicted to their phones than before.
Did you know that …?	**Did you know that** some companies monitor your phone?
The website says that …	**The website says that** elephants are in danger of disappearing.
According to …,	**According to** the BBC, the number one problem in the world is climate change.
They found that …	**They found that** the report was not true.

Showing increases and decreases	
increase/decrease	The price of milk keeps **increasing**.
go up/go down	The cost of traveling to Southeast Asia is **going down**.

61

Plan & Write

Use the information in "A Guide to Writing a Better Presentation" (p. 82) to plan and write your presentation. Also, see "A Guide to Creating Super Slides" (p. 86) to create great slides.

1. Decide your topic.

    My Topic _____

2. Brainstorm.

3. Decide your main idea or point.

    Example:
    - Plastic pollution is a major environmental problem. We can all do something to solve this problem.

4. Find stories, facts, and quotations, and write questions to use in your presentation.

5. Make an outline.

Introduction		Slides to use
Greet the audience.		*Slide with title and my name.*
Tell the audience what you will talk about.		
Say your main idea.		
Use a question, story, fact, or quotation.		

Body		Slides to use
Talk about your main points.		

Body	Slides to use
Give details about the topic.	
Give a reason for each of your opinions.	
Use a question, story, fact, or quotation.	

Conclusion	Slides to use
Give your final thoughts on the topic.	
State your main idea again.	
Thank the audience.	

Presentation Skills — Saying Numbers

When you report numbers and statistics in your presentation, it is important to say them correctly and clearly.

Activity

A Practice saying different types of numbers and statistics out loud.

Numbers	9,725	75,000	463,025	4,800,000
Large numbers	870 thousand 870,000	75 million 75,000,000	405 billion 405,000,000,000	17 trillion 17,000,000,000,000
Years & dates	by 1988	in the 1700s	from 300 BCE to 1100 CE	from the 19th to the 20th century
Fractions	one half 1/2	two thirds 2/3	five eighths 5/8	three quarters 3/4
Money	US$50 million	¥4.5 billion	€20,000,000	₩10B

B Work with a partner. Each student has a list of expressions with numbers. Do not look at each other's list. Student A says an expression and Student B writes it down. Then, Student B says an expression and Student A writes it down. Continue until you are finished both lists. Finally, check your answers.

Student A
a. 2 billion
b. In 1998
c. 13th century
d. US $70 million
e. 5.2%
f. 1/4
g. 1/3
h. In the 2000s
i. ¥4.3 billion
j. 25,500,000

Partner's Numbers
a. _____
b. _____
c. _____
d. _____
e. _____
f. _____
g. _____
h. _____
i. _____
j. _____

Student B
a. 75 million
b. In 2005
c. 5th century BCE
d. €200 billion
e. 42%
f. 3/4
g. 1/2
h. In the 1900s
i. ₩8.7 million
j. 8,200,000,000

Solving Problems Unit 7

Presentation Skills › Tables & Graphs

Tables and graphs are useful tools for displaying information in a slide or graphic. Below are examples of each type.

Tables show facts and compare different information.

	Canada	United States	Mexico
Population	36,290,000	323,100,000	127,500,000
Largest city & population	Toronto: 2,810,000	New York: 8,538,000	Mexico City: 12,294,000

Circle Graphs (Pie Charts) show percentages.

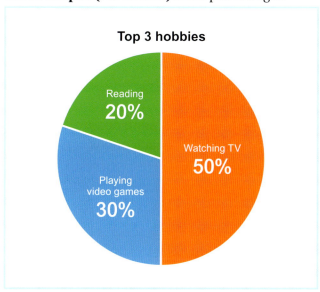

Line Graphs show changes over time.

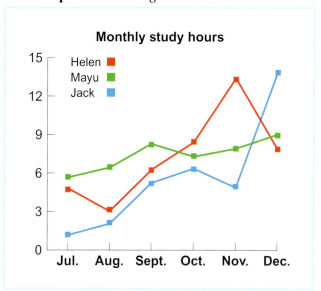

Vertical Bar Graphs show total numbers.

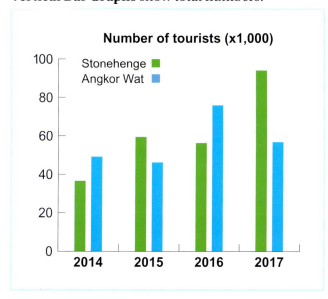

Horizontal Bar Graphs show speed or time.

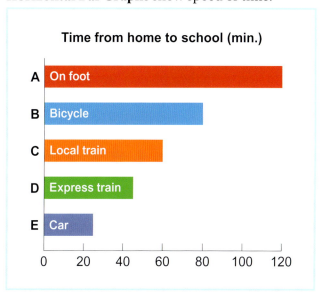

Presentation Skills — Chunking 1

English sentences can be divided into smaller sections. Each section expresses a piece of information. By chunking your writing, you will be able to deliver a clear presentation.

What is a chunk?

- A chunk is a group of words that communicates one piece of information.
- A chunk has one or two main words, and other words that are connected to them.

Main words:	nouns, verbs, adjectives, adverbs
Connecting words:	articles (a/an, the), prepositions (at, on, in, to, for, etc.), connectors (and, but, so, for, yet, etc.), modifiers (many, some, a few, much, etc.)

How to chunk?

- Divide sentences into chunks. Each chunk communicates one idea.
- Say the sentences out loud. **PAUSE briefly** after each chunk.

Activity

Chunk this introduction to a presentation about "Nomophobia." The first two sentences have been done for you. Then, practice it out loud, pausing briefly between each chunk.

> Nomophobia is increasing around the world. In fact, many people suffer from this sickness and don't know it. Why is nomophobia increasing? According to a website I read, people these days are starting to use mobile phones at younger and younger ages. They become addicted to their phones and can't live without them. For example, if they forget their phones at home, or if the battery dies, they feel very depressed. Surprisingly, some people go to sleep with their phones beside them. Personally, I think nomophobia is a serious problem and we should all stop using our mobile phones so much.

Make a Great Presentation

Use your notes from the "Plan & Write" pages and give a presentation about **a social or global issue that you are interested in**. After your presentation, use the "Self-Reflections" at the back of the book. What can you improve?

Unit 8

Final Presentation

You will give a final presentation based on a topic of your choice.

Share & Communicate

In a group or with a partner, discuss the questions and get ideas for your final presentation.

1. What place do you want to visit before you die?
2. Which historical person are you interested in knowing more about?
3. Who do you admire a lot?
4. What is a "perfect" day for you?
5. How important is music, art, or dance in your life?
6. What are you thankful for in your life?
7. What is most important for you in your life now?
8. What is one of your great accomplishments in life?
9. You have one year to do whatever you want. What do you do? Why?
10. What is one of your favorite places to visit?
11. Are sports important to you? Why or why not?
12. Your house or apartment catches fire. You can only save three items. What do you choose? Why?
13. Tell an interesting story that happened to you or someone you know.
14. What is one of your important goals for the next five years?
15. Is there a topic that you still want to do a presentation on?

Watch the Model Presentation

Watch the presenter talk about Africa and why she wants to go there.

If I had one wish, then I would like to travel to Africa, the place where modern human beings began about 200,000 years ago. Africa is a wonderful place to visit. It has great music, many different cultures, and gorgeous nature and wildlife. It is a place worth seeing!

One reason that I want to go to Africa is that I want to hear live music. African music is very lively and rhythmic. There are many kinds of African music, and each country has its own style. If I visit Africa, I must hear and dance to live music.

Next, I want to see and experience African nature. I want to see the African jungles, mountains, and the oceans, the lakes and the rivers. I especially want to see the famous Victoria Falls. I want to see elephants, zebras, lions, hippos, giraffes, rhinos, and cheetahs. Nowadays, there are many endangered species in Africa, and I want to see these animals in the wild, and not locked up in a zoo.

Finally, I want to communicate with the people. Africa has 54 countries, and each one is different. Their languages, history, customs, art, and music are all unique. I want to learn how the people live and think, and I want to understand more about their cultures.

So, I can sum up my presentation in one sentence: Before I die, I must travel to Africa, and hear live African music, see the beautiful nature and animals, and experience the many cultures there. One day, I will make this dream come true.

- wish「望み、願望」 ■ human beings「人類」 ■ gorgeous「すばらしい」 ■ wildlife「野生生物」
- place worth seeing「見る価値のある場所」 ■ lively「陽気な」 ■ zebra「シマウマ」 ■ hippo「カバ」
- giraffe「キリン」 ■ rhino「サイ」 ■ endangered species「絶滅危惧種」 ■ lock ... up「…を(檻に)閉じ込める」
- sum up ...「…をまとめる」 ■ make a dream come true「夢をかなえる」

Think! What topic do you want to focus on for your final presentation?

Final Presentation Unit 8

Plan & Write

Use the information in "A Guide to Writing a Better Presentation" (p. 82) to plan and write your presentation. Also, see "A Guide to Creating Super Slides" (p. 86) to create great slides.

1. Decide your topic.

   My Topic _____

2. Brainstorm.

3. Decide your main idea or point.

   Example:
   - Africa is a wonderful place to visit. Before I die, I must travel to Africa. I want to hear live African music, see the beautiful nature and animals, and experience the many cultures there.

4. Find stories, facts, and quotations, and write questions to use in your presentation.

5. Make an outline.

Introduction		Slides to use
Greet the audience.		Slide with title and my name.
Tell the audience what you will talk about.		
Say your main idea.		
Use a question, story, fact, or quotation.		

69

Body		Slides to use
Talk about your main points.		
Give details about the topic.		
Give a reason for each of your opinions.		

Final Presentation | Unit 8

Body		Slides to use
Give a reason for each of your opinions. *(Continued)*		
Use a question, story, fact, or quotation.		

Conclusion		Slides to use
Give your final thoughts on the topic.		
State your main idea again.		
Thank the audience.		

Presentation Skills > Chunking 2

Chunking can be used with emphasis to make your message easier for your audience to understand and follow.

Activity

Using the presentation on Africa, do the following:

1. Chunk the sentences into smaller parts. Then, choose 1 or 2 important words in each chunk and highlight them. The first paragraph has been done for you.

2. Practice reading the presentation out loud. Pause briefly between each chunk and emphasize the highlighted words by saying them louder.

If I had **one wish**, / then I would **like to travel** / to **Africa**, / the **place** / where **modern human beings began** / about **200,000 years** ago. / **Africa** is a **wonderful** place / to **visit**. / It has **great** music, / many **different** cultures, / and **gorgeous** nature / and **wildlife**. / It is a **place worth** seeing!

One reason that I want to go to Africa is that I want to hear live music. African music is very lively and rhythmic. There are many kinds of African music, and each country has its own style. If I visit Africa, I must hear and dance to live music.

Next, I want to see and experience African nature. I want to see the African jungles, mountains, and the oceans, the lakes and the rivers. I especially want to see the famous Victoria Falls. I want to see elephants, zebras, lions, hippos, giraffes, rhinos, and cheetahs. Nowadays, there are many endangered species in Africa, and I want to see these animals in the wild, and not locked up in a zoo.

Finally, I want to communicate with the people. Africa has 54 countries, and each one is different. Their languages, history, customs, art, and music are all unique. I want to learn how the people live and think, and I want to understand more about their cultures.

So, I can sum up my presentation in one sentence: Before I die, I must travel to Africa, and hear live African music, see the beautiful nature and animals, and experience the many cultures there. One day, I will make this dream come true.

Final Presentation — Unit 8

Gesture Review

With a partner, practice saying the phrases below and make the appropriate gestures. If you are not sure which gesture to use, ask your teacher. Then, watch the video to see examples.

Part 1

1. Now listen carefully!
2. We had a little bit of work to do.
3. There were only three people who came to the class.
4. I forgot to bring a pen for the test. I felt so stupid!
5. I was surprised to hear that.
6. First I flew to Hong Kong, and then I went to Bangkok.
7. The ticket prices kept getting higher.
8. On the one hand, I like this school. On the other hand, I wish they had a bigger campus.
9. I believe that we all will pass the test.
10. It was okay in the end.
11. What do YOU want to do after you graduate?

Part 2

1. My TOEIC score went down!
2. After that, I was very angry!
3. I didn't understand his Japanese.
4. I didn't like it and I told the young boy to stop.
5. It was not good at all!
6. I think this is very important!
7. I want everyone to join us.
8. The fish was very long.
9. I cried out, "Be careful!"
10. The room where I stayed was very cold at night.
11. I was really hoping to pass the test.

Final Summary

Here are the skills and tips that you have learned throughout this course. Review them and use as many as you can for your final presentation. Make a great presentation!

Before a presentation

1. Brainstorm ideas before you begin to plan and write your presentation.
2. Use outlines before you write the final copy.
3. Write according to the pattern of Introduction, Body, and Conclusion.
4. Practice several times to make sure you know your material well.
5. Stretch, breathe, and relax yourself before you do your presentation.
6. Think positive thoughts. Say something positive before you begin. For example, "This will be a great presentation." or "I will give a fantastic presentation."
7. Close your eyes and take a deep relaxing breath right before you begin to speak.

During a presentation

1. Speak loudly and clearly.
2. Make eye contact with the audience.
3. Use facial and hand gestures to express your message.
4. Stand or sit up straight. Keep your back straight throughout your presentation.
5. Use beautiful and clear slides to go with your talk.
6. Pause, and speak slowly to emphasize key words and expressions in your presentation.
7. Emphasize the important words in your message by saying them louder and with emotion.
8. Take a deep breath every once in a while to relax and slow yourself down.

After a presentation

1. Breathe deeply and smile. You did it!
2. Reflect on your presentation. What did you do well? What can you improve for the next presentation?

Make a Great Presentation

Use your notes from the "Plan & Write" pages and make your **final presentation**. After your presentation, use the "Self-Reflections" at the back of the book. What can you improve the next time you give a presentation?

Units 5–8 Review

A Read the story below about the Spanish painter, Pablo Picasso. Fill in the blanks with the words from the box.

According to	approximately	From	on
Although	As far as I'm concerned	in	to
and	but	known for	When

I love the Spanish artist Pablo Picasso. ^{1.}_____, he is the 20th century's greatest artist. Picasso was born in Spain ^{2.}_____ October 25, 1881. ^{3.}_____ Picasso was 16 years old, he went to Spain's top art college ^{4.}_____ he didn't finish his studies. In 1900, Picasso made his first trip to Paris which was the art capital of the world. ^{5.}_____ 1901 ^{6.}_____ 1920, Picasso developed many new styles of paintings ^{7.}_____ slowly, he became extremely rich and famous. ^{8.}_____ Picasso was famous because of his paintings, he was also ^{9.}_____ his sculpture. ^{10.}_____ his website, Picasso made ^{11.}_____ 50,000 artworks in his lifetime. Picasso died ^{12.}_____ 1973. I definitely believe that Pablo Picasso is one of the world's greatest artists.

B The skills below can be used before, during, and after a presentation. Read the sentences and write "before," "during," or "after" for each one. The first one has been done for you.

1. _before_   Decide your topic.
2. _____   Breathe deeply and smile! You did it!
3. _____   Brainstorm for ideas.
4. _____   Make good eye contact and use gestures.
5. _____   Practice several times.
6. _____   Speak loudly and clearly.
7. _____   Use the format of Introduction, Body, and Conclusion.
8. _____   Use larger images and a variety of font sizes on your slides.
9. _____   Relax yourself by breathing deeply and stretching.
10. _____   Create outlines to help write your final presentation.
11. _____   Think positive thoughts like, "I will give a great presentation."
12. _____   Have good posture.
13. _____   Use pauses and emphasize important words.
14. _____   Reflect on what you did well and how to improve.

C Match the statements (1–9) with the correct gestures (a–i).

1. We need to stop using our phones while eating!
2. First, I will tell you about her early life.
3. It costs a lot of money to travel for a year.
4. I hope I can reach my goal.
5. I didn't know what to do.
6. I was angry because someone stole my passport!
7. There were many small fish in the pond.
8. On the one hand, I want to live in another country. On the other hand, I like where I live.
9. What do YOU think of this problem?'

A Guide to Vocal Warm-ups

Your voice is like any muscle in your body. You need to warm it up before you give a presentation, so you can speak loudly and clearly.

Read the list of words, from top to bottom, as clearly and loudly as you can.

1.

Oooh ooh ooh	Ah ah ah	Up up up	Look look look
Eee eee eee	It it it	Cat cat cat	No no no!
Oooh ooh ooh	Ah ah ah	Up up up	Look look look
Eee eee eee	It it it	Cat cat cat	No no no!

2.

She she she saw saw saw a ship ship ship
On the lake lake lake late at night night night
She she she saw saw saw a ship ship ship
On the lake lake lake late at night night night

3.

Bo do fo go ho	Pah rah sah tah nah
Bo do fo go ho	Pah rah sah tah nah
Kee lee mee nee fee	Voo woo yoo zoo shoo
Kee lee mee nee fee	Voo woo yoo zoo shoo

4.

Pa pa pa	Fit fit fit	Zoo zoo zoo
Ba ba ba	Vit vit vit	Zyoo zyoo zyoo
Ta ta ta	Mit mit mit	This this this
Da da da	Nit nit nit	Third third third
Ko ko ko	See see see	Hood hood hood
Go go go	Shee shee shee	Wood wood wood
Ro ro ro	Chee chee chee	Sing sing song
Lo lo lo	Jee jee jee	Yay sayonara

A Guide to Better Pronunciation › Consonant & Vowel Sounds

Speaking clearly is very important when giving presentations. Saying the sentences below is good practice because it helps you improve your pronunciation, intonation, and enunciation.

Consonant Sounds

1. **p/b**
   Peter **b**rought **b**oxes of **p**opcorn to the **b**irthday **p**arty. **B**ravo **P**eter!

2. **t/d**
   Tim said the **d**owntown got ho**tt**er and ho**tt**er **d**uring the **d**ust storm.

3. **k/g**
   Kathy's **k**ite fell on the **g**reen **g**rass while the other **g**irls **g**ig**g**led.

4. **r/l**
   Shei**l**a **r**eceived **r**eal **r**ed **r**oses.
   The poo**r p**i**l**ot sat by the poo**l** and **l**aughed **r**eally **l**oudly.
   I **l**ike **fr**esh**l**y **fr**ied **fr**esh **fl**at **f**ish very much.

5. **f/v**
   Victoria loves **v**iewing the **f**ifty-**f**ive **f**oxes that are li**v**ing in the **f**ields.
   For her **v**ictory, she recei**v**ed a lo**v**ely **v**ase with **f**orty-**f**our **f**lowers.

6. **n/m**
   Mary bought **m**any **n**ew su**mm**er swi**m**suits.
   No, **n**o, **n**o, **n**o, **n**ot **n**ow!

7. **s/sh**
   She **s**urely know**s** how to **s**ell **s**ea**sh**ells, doesn't **sh**e?
   There were **s**eventy-**s**even **s**ick **f**i**sh**ermen **s**ailing on a **s**ea **sh**ip.

8. **ch/j**
   Chuck says there are **ch**ubby **j**ugglers in the kit**ch**en with **J**ane.

9. **ʒ/z**
   I u**s**ually spend my lei**s**ure time in A**s**ia.
   There are A**s**ian elephants and African **z**ebras in the **z**oo.

10. **θ/ð**
    He **th**rew **th**irty-**th**ree free **th**rows on **Th**ursday.
    The birthday party is on **th**e **th**ird, four**th**, and fif**th** floors.

11. **h/w**
    Harry **h**id **h**is **h**at as **h**e **h**eld the **h**orse.
    The **w**oman in the **w**oods **h**as **w**olves as pets.
    What **w**onderful **w**eather!

12. **ng**
    Mi**ng** sa**ng** a so**ng** for the ki**ng**.

13. **y**
   I bought **y**ummy **y**ellow **y**ams and **y**uzu.
   You **y**odeled beautifully **y**esterday.

Vowel Sounds

1. /i/ as in s**ee**
   The refer**ee** didn't s**ee** so w**e** didn't get a fr**ee** kick.

2. /ɪ/ as in f**i**t
   I **i**magine **I** w**i**ll never get f**i**t **i**f my d**i**et **i**sn't f**i**xed.
   Is **i**t **i**mportant for the Br**i**tish ch**i**ldren to do **i**t today?

3. /ɛ/ as in **e**ver
   I have n**e**ver **e**ver seen th**e**m tog**e**ther exc**e**pt at the w**e**dding.
   She s**e**nt her b**e**st fri**e**nd a l**e**tter but it w**e**nt to the wrong addr**e**ss.

4. /æ/ as in d**a**d
   My d**a**d h**a**s a pl**a**n to tr**a**vel to Fr**a**nce **a**nd C**a**nada with his c**a**t **a**nd a b**a**ckp**a**ck.

5. /ɑ/ as in rob**o**t
   We can n**o**t keep the rob**o**t on the y**a**cht that we b**ou**ght.

6. /ɔ/ as in w**a**lk
   Grandpa w**a**lked and t**a**lked as he th**ou**ght about the new l**a**w.
   He s**a**w me dr**a**w a jigs**a**w in the h**a**ll.

7. /ʊ/ as in b**oo**k
   He read a b**oo**k about a c**oo**k who c**oo**ked baref**oo**t.
   Don't l**oo**k at the outp**u**t or the inp**u**t.

8. /u/ as in y**ou**
   D**o** y**ou** want t**o** try a f**ew** of the n**ew** cash**ew**s?
   Tw**o** members of the cr**ew** ate fond**ue** as the plane fl**ew** itself.

9. /ʌ/ as in l**o**ve
   He was in l**o**ve with the c**ou**sin of the man **u**pstairs.
   My c**ou**sin loves doing sit **u**ps and push **u**ps in fr**o**nt of the TV.

10. /ə/ as in camp**u**s
    Th**e** president likes to c**e**lebrate by eating th**e** pizz**a** they serve at th**e** plaz**a**.
    Th**e** transportati**o**n on camp**u**s was th**e** best.

11. /eɪ/ as in b**ay**
    The caf**é** by the b**ay** m**ay** be open at midd**ay**, but the staff m**ay** be del**ay**ed by l**a**te subw**ay** tr**ai**ns.
    Th**ey** st**ay**ed at the caf**é** and m**a**de plans to m**a**ke a displ**ay** for the subw**ay**.

12. /aɪ/ as in f**i**ve
    I finally found the f**i**ve videos of the l**i**ve concert.
    The w**i**ves are dr**i**ving to Tokyo Sk**y**tree, but they haven't arr**i**ved yet.

13. /ɔɪ/ as in b**oy**
    The b**oy** was filled with j**oy** when he got a t**oy** cowb**oy**.
    The schoolb**oy** said in a loud v**oi**ce, "I enj**oy** eating s**oy** beans."

14. /aʊ/ as in h**ow**
    Someh**ow** I will find **ou**t h**ow** he was all**ow**ed into Mac**au**.

15. /oʊ/ as in g**o**
    Could you g**o** and take a ph**oto** of the potat**o**es behind the pati**o** tomorr**ow**?
    I listened to the stere**o** as I made a tomat**o** risott**o**, while sipping sl**ow**ly on an espress**o**.

16. /ər/ as in sist**er**
    His sist**er** was a doct**or**, while his broth**er** was a wait**er**.

17. /ɜr/ as in w**or**d
    The th**ir**d p**er**son has to write a w**or**d that rhymes with sh**ir**t.
    The entrepren**eur** went **ear**ly to w**or**k on Th**ur**sday.

18. /ɪr/ as in b**eer**
    The engin**eer** drank b**eer** with the cash**ier** from the volunt**eer** group.
    It isn't cl**ear** why the d**eer** have disapp**ear**ed.

19. /ɛr/ as in b**ear**
    I was sc**are**d of the b**ear** that entered the f**air**.
    In my nightm**are**, I cut the h**air** of a p**air** of r**are** b**ear**s upst**air**s.

20. /ɑr/ as in c**ar**
    The c**ar** p**ar**k for the cig**ar** b**ar** was f**ar** from the streetc**ar** stop.
    The l**ar**ge cavi**ar** j**ar** on the b**ar** looked just like a cookie j**ar**.

21. /ɔr/ as in d**oor**
    Y**our** friend has a s**ore** toe because he kicked the dr**awer** as well as the d**oor** at the bookst**ore**.
    I put y**our** dinos**aur**s in the dr**awer** nearest the fl**oor**.

22. /ʊr/ as in t**our**
    The t**our** bus driver was uns**ure** but he still followed the det**our**.
    I made s**ure** that we had ins**ur**ance for the t**our**.

A Guide to Better Pronunciation — Classic Tongue Twisters

Tongue twisters are very good for practicing how to say English sounds clearly. They also help with enunciation. For the tongue twisters below, do not try to say them quickly, but try to enunciate. To enunciate is to say words as clearly as possible.

65–74

1. She sells seashells down by the seashore.
2. Which wristwatch is a Swiss wristwatch?
3. How much wood would a woodchuck chuck
   If a woodchuck could chuck wood?
   He would chuck as much wood
   As a woodchuck could
   If a woodchuck could chuck wood.
4. Peter Piper picked a peck of pickled peppers.
   Did Peter Piper pick a peck of pickled peppers?
   If Peter Piper picked a peck of pickled peppers,
   Where's the pickled peppers Peter Piper picked?
5. Red lorry, yellow lorry.
6. A tutor who tooted the flute
   Tried to tutor two tutors to toot
   Said the two to the tutor
   "Is it harder to toot
   Or tutor two tutors to toot?"
7. If two witches watched two watches,
   Which witch watched which watch?
8. A swan swam over the swell
   "Swim swan swim."
   The swan swam back through the swell
   "Well-swum swan."
9. Betty Botter bought some butter.
   "But," she said, "this butter's bitter.
   If I put it in my batter,
   It will make my batter bitter.
   But a bit of better butter,
   That will make my batter better."
   So she bought a bit of butter
   Better than her bitter butter,
   And she put it in her batter
   And the batter was not bitter.
   So 'twas better Betty Botter
   Bought a bit of better butter.
10. I scream, you scream, we all scream for ice cream.

A Guide to Writing a Better Presentation

Good presenters always plan carefully. In this section, you will be guided through a good example of planning, preparing, and writing your presentation.

1. **Decide your topic.** Find a topic you are interested in.

2. **Brainstorm.** Think of ideas or points you want to talk about. You can simply think about them or write them down on a piece of paper. You do not have to write sentences. You can write only words and use drawings or tables.

3. **Decide your main idea or point.** Try to summarize your main idea in 1–3 sentences.

    Examples:
    - The most important person in my life is my mother because she supports me whenever I have troubles. She is my best friend.
    - I love musicals because there is so much to see and hear. Musicals have acting, singing, dancing, and a great story.

4. **Use questions, stories, facts, and quotations.** Use some of the following techniques for your presentation.

    a. **Ask a question.** A good way to catch the audience's attention is to ask a question.

    Examples:
    - What did you do before you came to this school?
    - Have you ever …?
    - Did you know that …?

    b. **Tell a story.** People like to hear stories. In your presentation, you can use a personal story, a story from someone else's life, or an interesting story from the news.

    Example:
    - I will begin with a story that happened to me last week. I was sitting in a café when …

    c. **Use facts.** A fact is a statistic or piece of information that is true. Facts make your presentation powerful and interesting. Facts can come from the Internet, newspapers, magazines, or books. Be sure to check that the facts are correct.

    Example:
    - In Japan, more than 50% of high school graduates go to university or college.

    d. **Use a quotation.** A quotation is a popular saying or proverb, or the words from a poem, song, or person.

    Example:
    - A popular saying is, "Once a year, go someplace you have never been before." I strongly agree with this.

5. **Make an outline**. Make an outline for the points you will talk about. Use the following presentation format: **Introduction, Body, Conclusion.**

INTRODUCTION
   a. The presenter greets the audience.
   b. The presenter introduces the main theme of the presentation and tells the audience what he/she will talk about.
   c. The presenter says the main idea of the presentation.

BODY
   a. The presenter talks about the main points of the presentation.
   b. There should be reasons or explanations for opinion statements.
   c. You can make this section interesting by using questions, stories, quotations, facts, and opinions.

CONCLUSION
   a. The presenter gives final thoughts on the topic.
   b. The presenter repeats the main idea of the presentation.
   c. The presenter thanks the audience for listening.

After you have finished writing your notes or first draft of your presentation, it is good to check for ways to improve your writing. Use the questions below to help improve your writing.

1. Are your main ideas clear and easy to understand?
2. Do you use examples, facts, statistics, or stories to make your main idea clearer?
3. Do you support your opinions with reasons?

Structure

1. Do you have an introduction, body, and conclusion?
2. Do you say your main idea in the introduction and the conclusion?
   - Introduction: Say what your main idea is.
   - Body: Support your main idea with examples, stories, facts, and statistics.
   - Conclusion: Say your main idea one more time.
3. Can you improve the introduction or conclusion?

Grammar

1. Are the verb tenses used correctly? Did you use the past, present, and future tenses correctly?
   - Wrong: Yesterday, we **go** to the new museum.
   - Correct: Yesterday, we **went** to the new museum.
2. Do the subjects and verbs agree?
   - Wrong: She **go** to school every Monday.
   - Correct: She **goes** to school every Monday.
3. Did you use the articles "a", "an", and "the'" correctly?

Vocabulary & Pronunciation

1. Do you use some words too often? If so, use synonyms—similar words in meaning. You can use an online thesaurus to help you.
2. Did you check vocabulary that you are not sure of?
3. Did you check the pronunciation of the words that you will say out loud during your presentation?

A Guide to Using Notes

Some presenters memorize their presentations. Others use the "Read, Look Up, Present" technique with their script. But another way to give a presentation is to use **notes.**

Notes are pieces of paper that have the most important points, key words, and expressions written on them. They help the presenter remember the order of the main points.

Look at the example on the next page. They are notes for the Self-Introduction presentation in Unit 1.

Hello everyone. My name is Mayu but my nickname is Maggie. Please call me Maggie.

1. **Introduction**
   - greeting
   - name—nickname
   - call me Maggie

First, let me begin by talking about my background and family. I was born in Yokote in Akita. I love the winter there because we can go skiing a lot. Anyway, I have a big family. I have two sisters, my parents, and a beautiful Shiba-inu called Snoopy. My father works in China now and my mother works part-time. My sisters are high school students. We all get along well.

2. **Background**
   - born in
   - skiing in winter
   - family + Snoopy
   - father/mother's work
   - sisters—get along well

Next, I'll talk about my school life. I'm an English major at school. I love all of my classes, especially my communication ones. At school, I also belong to the glee club because I love singing.

3. **School**
   - major
   - love all classes
   - glee club member
   - love singing

Finally, I'll tell you what I like to do in my free time. Well, I like to go out with my friends, watch movies, and surf the Internet. I also work part-time in a karaoke shop. I love food and so, I really enjoy cooking for my family. I especially like making curries.

4. **Free Time**
   - go out with friends, movies, surf the Internet
   - part-time job
   - cooking for family

So, now you know more about me. I hope you enjoyed my talk. I'm really looking forward to this presentation class. Thank you.

5. **Conclusion**
   - now you know
   - I hope you enjoyed
   - looking forward to
   - Thank you

A Guide to Creating Super Slides

It is important to design slides that make your presentations exciting and easier for the audience to remember.

Why use slides?

Slides add a visual dimension to your presentation and create an emotional reaction in your audience.

Well-designed slides make the message of your presentation deeper and more powerful.

Making super slides

It takes a lot of time to make a super slide.

There are five important areas to think about when you design your super slides.

1 Text

Don't write too much text on your slide. Your audience will NOT listen to you. They will read the slide. This slide has too much text.

- Paris is called the City of Lights.
- There are over 296 illuminated sites in Paris: hotels, churches, statues, fountains, and national buildings and monuments.
- 33 of Paris' 37 bridges are illuminated at nightfall.
- The Eiffel Tower uses 20,000 light bulbs and 40 km of cable to light up this famous Paris landmark.
- Paris was the birthplace of the "Age of Enlightenment" and was a famous center for education and ideas throughout Europe.
- Paris' early adoption of street lighting contributed to its "City of Lights" nickname.

The 3 x 6 rule. Use the 3 x 6 rule when writing text on your slide:

- Limit text to a maximum of **3 lines** per slide and **6 words** per line.
- Don't write full sentences.
- Use keywords or short phrases only.

These slides have the same information as the slide on the previous page, but they follow the 3 x 6 rule.

- Paris—City of Lights
- 296 illuminated sites
- 33 illuminated bridges

- Eiffel Tower—20,000 light bulbs
- Age of Enlightenment center
- First city to use street lights

2 Fonts & Font sizes

A font is the style of printed type. There are three types of fonts.

Serif fonts have small "hooks" on the ends of the letters.

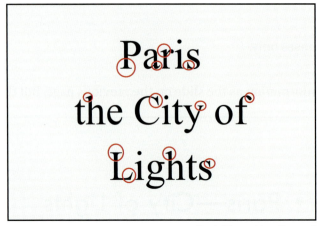

(font: Times New Roman)

Sans Serif fonts don't have hooks on the letters. They are simple.

Paris the City of Lights

(font: Open Sans)

Script fonts look like handwriting.

Paris the City of Lights

(font: Dancing Script)

A Guide to Creating Super Slides

To make your text look interesting, use the following design tips:

Use large font sizes. People at the back of the room should be able to read the words easily. Font sizes should be **30 points or bigger.**

Use 2 (not 3) font types. By using 2 font types, your slide looks more interesting to the audience.

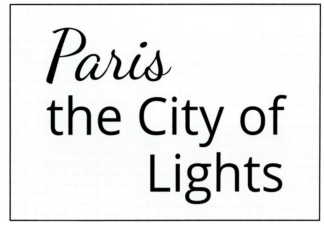

(fonts: Dancing Script & Open Sans)

Use different font sizes and make the keywords bigger. By making the keywords on the slide bigger, the audience can easily understand the key point of your message.

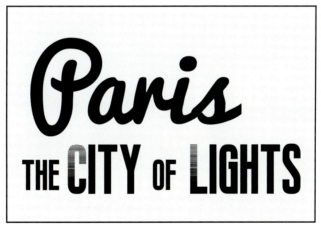

(fonts: Pacifico & BOXING)

Don't use "boring" fonts. Find interesting and unique fonts for your slides. Don't use fonts that are used often in documents. If possible, download free fonts from the Internet and make your slides look more interesting.

3 Color & Contrast

People love to see colors. If you use colors well, they will make your slides look more attractive. Every good slide designer should know what contrasting colors are and how to use them.

Colors create emotion. Color communicates emotion to the audience. Choose colors that match the mood of your presentation.

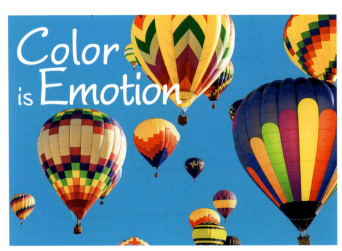

Contrast. Use contrasting colors between the text and the background. This makes your slides easy to see.

- **Good contrast:** Light text against a dark background.

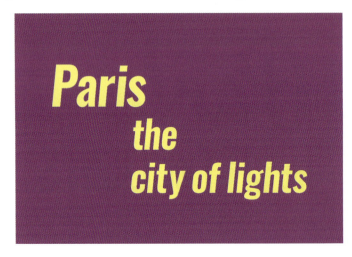

- **Good contrast:** Dark text against a light background.

- **Bad contrast:** Light text against a light background.

Paris *the* **city of lights**

- **Don't be too colorful:** Too many colors make it difficult to look at the slide.

Paris *the* **city of lights**

Use the color wheel. A color wheel will help you choose colors for your slides. Use primary colors (red, blue, yellow) for excitement. Contrast the primary color with the secondary color across from it in the color wheel (red–green, blue–orange, yellow–purple). Contrasting colors are also attractive to the eye.

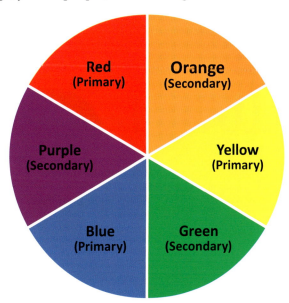

91

4 Images & Illustrations

People remember pictures longer than words. If you use words together with images or illustrations, the audience will remember your presentation longer.

Use these tips to choose images for your presentations:

Use large images. Fill the whole slide with an image.

IMPORTANT! Images should be 1,200 pixels x 800 pixels or bigger. If they are smaller, they will look bad on the screen.

Match your words with an image. What is the main point you want people to remember? What image connects to that idea?

Use images to make your audience "think" or "feel" something. A good presentation connects "emotionally" with the audience.

Choose images that create emotions. If you use an image that makes you feel happy, sad, excited, or angry, your audience will feel that way too.

Illustrations. Illustrations can be just as effective for catching the audience's attention. Use your imagination and draw your own illustrations if you can.

IMPORTANT! Don't use copyrighted images and illustrations. Use the Creative Commons search feature when you search on the Internet.

5 Design

People understand a presentation better if the words are supported with well-designed slides. The guidelines below will help you design slides that communicate emotionally with the audience.

The 5-Second Rule. The audience should understand the slide in 5 seconds.

Use the Rule of Thirds. Divide the slide evenly into nine sections. Look at the diagram below. Put the strongest part of the image or the key text at one of the points where the lines cross. These points are where people look automatically.

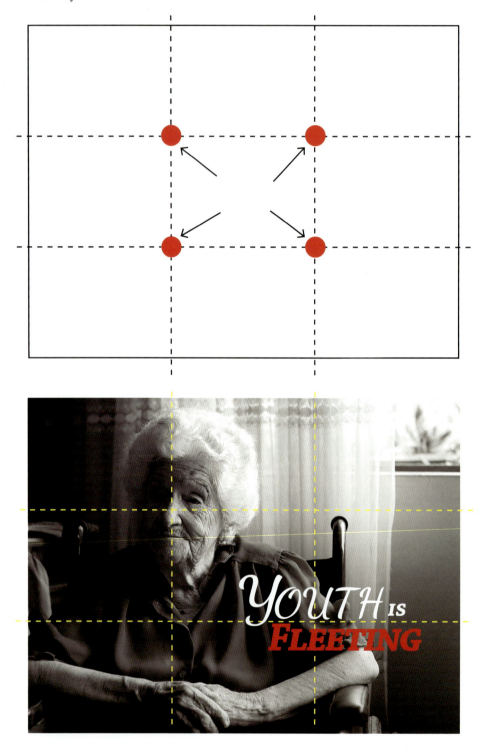

One slide, one idea. Each slide should communicate only one idea.

Use empty (negative) space. Put your text in the empty part of the image.

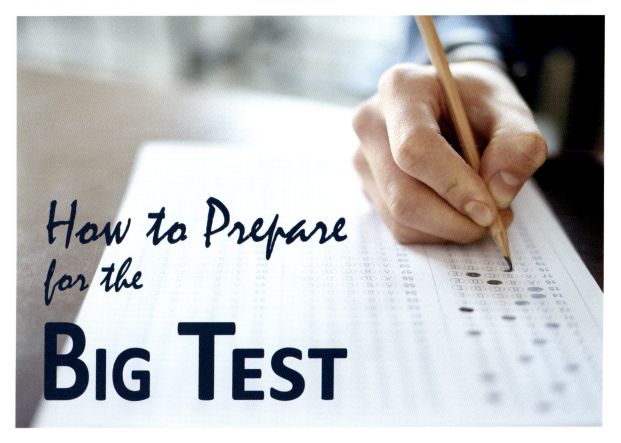

Use shapes. Squares, circles, triangles, and arrows help the audience see your message clearly.

Use quotations. Use quotations to support an idea or your main theme.

Rotate text for effect. Sometimes, change the angle of the text. This makes your slide more interesting.

Don't use small images. Your audience will not be able to see the content of the slide very well.

Don't use too many images. If you use too many images on one slide, the audience will be distracted.

A Guide to Class Warm-ups & Relaxation

It is important to be relaxed when you give a presentation. These activities will help you get ready to give a great presentation.

Activity A

This is a good activity for practicing good posture. Watch the video to see a demonstration.

1. Stand up.
2. Put your feet shoulder length apart. Keep your hands at your side.
3. Pull up your shoulders as high as you can. Then let them fall down. Repeat.
4. Twist the upper part of your body to the right. Hold it. Bring it back. Repeat.
5. Twist the upper part of your body to the left. Hold it. Bring it back. Repeat.
6. Lift up both heels of your feet. Hold them up for 10 seconds. Repeat.
7. Close your eyes and take two long, deep breaths.
8. Open your eyes and smile.

Activity B

This is an interesting activity for practicing good posture. Watch the video to see a demonstration.

1. Stand up.
2. Put your feet shoulder length apart. Keep your hands at your side.
3. Twist your head to the right. Hold it. Bring it back. Repeat.
4. Twist your head to the left. Bring it back. Repeat.
5. Put your hands up in the air. Stand up on your toes. Reach for the sky. Repeat.
6. Shake your arms and hands.
7. Put your right arm straight out to the side with your palm up. Bring your arm up over your head. Repeat.
8. Put your left arm straight out to the side with your palm up. Bring your arm up over your head. Repeat.
9. Bend your knees and bring your body down as far as you can. Repeat.
10. Close your eyes and take a long, deep breath. Repeat.
11. Open your eyes and smile.

A Guide to Presentation Self-Reflections

Use these tables to reflect on each of your presentations. Check (✓) the answer that best describes you.

Unit 1: Self-Introduction

How did you do with the points below?	This was difficult for me.	I thought I did fine.	I want to improve this.
Planning & writing an outline			
Writing the presentation, or creating notes			
Making good eye contact			
Voice control			
Relaxing during my presentation			

Unit 2: An Important Person or Thing

My Topic _____

How did you do with the points below?	This was difficult for me.	I thought I did fine.	I want to improve this.
Planning & writing an outline			
Writing the presentation, or creating notes			
Content or message of my presentation			
Making good eye contact			
Voice control			
Good posture			
Relaxing during my presentation			
Using facial gestures			
Using hand gestures			
Using my notes: "Read, Look Up, Present"			

Unit 3: Places

My Topic _____

How did you do with the points below?	This was difficult for me.	I thought I did fine.	I want to improve this.
Planning & writing an outline			
Writing the presentation, or creating notes			
Content or message of my presentation			
Making good eye contact			
Voice control			
Good posture			
Relaxing during my presentation			
Using facial gestures			
Using hand gestures			
Using my notes: "Read, Look Up, Present"			
Creating super slides			

Unit 4: Opinions

My Topic _____

How did you do with the points below?	This was difficult for me.	I thought I did fine.	I want to improve this.
Planning & writing an outline			
Writing the presentation, or creating notes			
Content or message of my presentation			
Making good eye contact			
Voice control			
Good posture			
Relaxing during my presentation			
Using facial gestures			
Using hand gestures			
Using my notes: "Read, Look Up, Present"			

Unit 5: Biography

My Topic _____

How did you do with the points below?	This was difficult for me.	I thought I did fine.	I want to improve this.
Planning & writing an outline			
Writing the presentation, or creating notes			
Content or message of my presentation			
Making good eye contact			
Voice control			
Good posture			
Relaxing during my presentation			
Using facial gestures			
Using hand gestures			
Using my notes: "Read, Look Up, Present"			
Creating super slides			

Unit 6: Stories

My Topic _____

How did you do with the points below?	This was difficult for me.	I thought I did fine.	I want to improve this.
Planning & writing an outline			
Writing the presentation, or creating notes			
Content or message of my presentation			
Making good eye contact			
Voice control			
Good posture			
Relaxing during my presentation			
Using facial gestures			
Using hand gestures			
Using my notes: "Read, Look Up, Present"			

A Guide to Presentation Self-Reflections

Unit 7: Solving Problems

My Topic _____

How did you do with the points below?	This was difficult for me.	I thought I did fine.	I want to improve this.
Planning & writing an outline			
Writing the presentation, or creating notes			
Content or message of my presentation			
Making good eye contact			
Voice control			
Good posture			
Relaxing during my presentation			
Using facial gestures			
Using hand gestures			
Using my notes: "Read, Look Up, Present"			
Creating super slides			

Unit 8: Final Presentation

My Topic _____

How did you do with the points below?	This was difficult for me.	I thought I did fine.	I want to improve this.
Planning & writing an outline			
Writing the presentation, or creating notes			
Content or message of my presentation			
Making good eye contact			
Voice control			
Good posture			
Relaxing during my presentation			
Using facial gestures			
Using hand gestures			
Using my notes: "Read, Look Up, Present"			
Creating super slides			

クラス用DVD有り(別売)
クラス用音声CD有り(別売)

Ready to Present—A Guide to Better Presentations

2019年3月20日　初版発行
2023年8月20日　第 7 刷

著　者　　Herman Bartelen、Malcolm Kostiuk
発行者　　松村達生
発行所　　センゲージ ラーニング株式会社
　　　　　〒102-0073　東京都千代田区九段北1-11-11　第2フナトビル5階
　　　　　電話 03-3511-4392　FAX 03-3511-4391
　　　　　e-mail: eltjapan@cengage.com
　　　　　copyright©2019 センゲージ ラーニング株式会社

装　丁　　足立友幸(parastyle)
制作協力　飯尾緑子(parastyle)
映像制作　高速録音株式会社
印刷・製本　株式会社ムレコミュニケーションズ

ISBN 978-4-86312-351-9

もし落丁、乱丁、その他不良品がありましたら、お取り替えいたします。本書の全部、または一部を無断で複写(コピー)することは、著作権法上での例外を除き、禁じられていますのでご注意ください。